ADVANCED DRIVER

ADVANCED DRIVER

Joe Kells

DAVID & CHARLES
NEWTON ABBOT   LONDON   NORTH POMFRET (VT)   VANCOUVER

British Library Cataloguing in Publication Data

Kells, Joseph
   Advanced driver.
   1. Automobile driving
   I. Title
   629.28'3'2   TL152.5

   ISBN 0-7153-7494-X

© Joe Kells 1978

Set in 'Compugraphic' Baskerville and printed in
Great Britain by Biddles Ltd Guildford Surrey
for David & Charles (Publishers) Limited
Brunel House   Newton Abbot   Devon

Published in the United States of America
by David & Charles Inc
North Pomfret   Vermont 05053   USA

Published in Canada
by Douglas David & Charles Limited
1875 Welch Street   North Vancouver   BC

Contents

CHAPTER ONE

What is 'Advanced Driving'?

To the modern motorist there is a significant sign beside Grove Hill, Harrow. It marks the site of the first fatal car accident in Great Britain, on 22 February 1899. At that time, as a result of the 'Emancipation Act', the maximum speed limit was 12 mph, so it would be interesting to know the nature and cause of the accident.[1]

The very word 'accident' implies something which could not be avoided and is therefore a misnomer for the incidents that occur on our roads today. A more accurate word would be 'collision', and these don't just happen, they are caused — usually by one driver.

Three things are necessary for a collision — roads, vehicles and drivers. Weather conditions may also possibly contribute.

Although roads in Britain still leave a great deal to be desired, there is always one driver concerned in a collision who failed to take into account the poor road conditions and therefore adjust his course and speed accordingly. That driver is therefore blameworthy, *not* the vehicle, the road, or the weather. Vehicles are often blamed for being defective, but any thinking driver will agree that defects which could have not been foreseen and prevented by good maintenance are extremely rare. Hence a driver who knowingly takes a defective vehicle on the road is criminally negligent, irresponsible and quite obviously the guilty party in any resulting collision.

Potential collision conditions constantly recur in dense traffic, and are only prevented from resulting in disaster by either good fortune or the skill and adroitness of other drivers. Hence it follows that in the vast majority of collisions there is a deficiency of driver education — somewhere.

In the current Department of Transport L test, a candidate's actual driving time may be as little as thirty minutes. This is manifestly insufficient for the assessment of consideration, concentration and consistent competency during any realistic journey through contemporary traffic. Besides, a candidate is naturally on his best behaviour in the presence of an examiner; even a novice can usually suppress latent faults for short periods. Herein lies the main advantage of Advanced Tests. The fact that nearly everybody is prepared to pay a high price *after* an 'accident' and not before one is as good a reason as any for facing up to the fact that prevention is still better than cure. We should all be prepared to pay a very much higher price for safety on the road. Admittedly there is no such thing as absolute safety, but a tremendous amount can still be done in the training and re-training of drivers.

There must be something wrong with our system when a young man under twenty-five, who becomes a responsible citizen in later years, and who now has very fast reactions enabling him to be among the best drivers on the road has the worst 'accident' record and is therefore penalised by insurance companies. His driving education was not complete, or these companies would not have to impose such high premiums. As the matter stands today, he is allowed to gain driving maturity only at the cost of experience, which can often prove expensive in damage and injuries.

The mechanical skills of car driving are so very simple that they encourage over-confidence, but a car is a precision vehicle which can be lethal in inexperienced or irresponsible hands. Any member of the population who can satisfy an examiner that he is able to drive unaccompanied is allowed to do so, and often in very difficult conditions. (The L test is cancelled if the weather is bad, and there is no motorway driving, night driving or any other reasonable test to prove a candidate's competence to cope with other than ideal conditions.) A novice driver's pass certificate can at once be exchanged for a full driving licence. As a rule he then drives happily around this country and others, where the laws and highway procedure differ considerably from our own, for the next umpteen years — possibly in a high powered vehicle, and often with his car in top gear and his mind in neutral, under the fond delusion that he knows it all.

The mere fact that a single driving test is sufficient to carry a driver through from the age of seventeen to seventy-plus is, in our increasing traffic density, quite preposterous. Improved vehicle performance also complicates the problem for the more inexperienced. After all, doctors, dentists, engineers and other professionals continue their education beyond the point of minimum qualification. So should drivers. Responsible ones already do so.

As an illustration of just what loopholes there are in our motoring laws, it is still legal for those who held a licence before 1 January 1935, and who have never in their lives passed a driving test, to drive on the public roads. As a direct result of this there are a great many drivers of advanced age on the roads today whose competence has never been tested, and who would certainly fail. In addition, holders of current licences who have not driven for perhaps more than a decade are legally qualified to do so provided they regularly renew their original licences. Such people can be quite charming companions, and may even discourse knowledgeably about motoring, blandly announcing: 'Never had an accident in me

9

life, old boy'. One wonders, though, just how many they might have caused.

Good driving is a result of continual *conscious* practice, and a very simple summary of it is this: always try to be in the correct gear, at the correct speed, in the correct lane at the proper time for any manoeuvre — *after* first having checked that it is perfectly safe to carry out that manoeuvre and signalled your intention to do so. *Any one* of the factors just mentioned, if omitted from your customary and normal drill, could result in a collision.

There are many drivers on the roads today who consider themselves, not without good reason, to be very skilled indeed, but this is not all there is to being a 'good' driver. One can be skilled without having consideration for others, and this could be, and sometimes is, fatal. Here is an example:

> an elderly and somewhat nervous person is driving a small family saloon along a safe main road at a sedate speed. There is a T junction ahead on the left hand side. Suddenly our driver sights a sports car coming fast along the side road on the left with the obvious intention of turning out into the main road. He is moving at considerable speed, and our driver begins to wonder whether in fact the sports car even intends to stop at the junction. The sports car driver is in fact a highly skilled rally driver, not accustomed to taking uncalculated risks, but our driver is not to know that. The sports car driver does in fact brake, but hard and late, as competition drivers often do. Unfortunately by the time he does so our nervous driver has panicked, swerved, and perhaps even induced a heart condition, at least, in other drivers of oncoming traffic. A skid could result, and one or more collisions.

This would never have occurred if the sports car driver had exercised some degree of responsibility towards other road users and approached the junction at a less alarming speed.

10

The fact that he belonged to a band of the most skilful drivers in the world, although of great use in keeping him out of accidents, would be an absolute menace if it caused alarm and despondency in other people. There is a time and place for handbrake turns, the use of high speed, slides, drifts, broadsides and so on, but it is *not* on the public roads. It is for precisely this reason that racetracks, autocross courses, skidpans and so forth exist.

The best and most responsible drivers are those who drive with both skill and restraint, and who, in the course of their everyday driving, show good manners. The advanced driver sets an example in this, and permits nothing whatever to interfere with his concentration whilst he is at the wheel.

It has already been emphasised that the major cause of collisions is human error, and that the infallible driver is a rarity. In fact he is so rare that he doesn't even exist. This, however, is a negative statement. The fact that he doesn't yet exist leaves the field wide open for you. It is up to you to strive towards becoming the best driver in at least your own neighbourhood.

If you watch any sportsman in the 'star' class you will see that he appears to have ample time to deal with almost any eventuality; he makes it all seem so very simple. But when you try the same thing chaos inevitably results. His was not just the outcome of being a born golfer/swimmer/footballer/boxer, but the deserved product of a great many hours of concentration and assiduous practice. Unfortunately the vast majority of drivers, when they achieve the dignity of a full driving licence, rarely bother with any more practice at all. One of the reasons quoted is that the greatly increased cost of motoring allows only essential trips. This argument, although very understandable in the light of our current finances, is one which in reality betrays false economy, for, compared with the cost of a collision in monetary and human suffering, the cost of fuel is negligible.

11

Many aspects of road safety are controversial. The community is at present faced with an annual bill of something like £250 million as a direct result of road accidents. It would therefore seem that we are not yet prepared to pay an individual price for their reduction. Blaming the government which happens to be in power for any failure to improve roads is farcical if we, as drivers, are not prepared to contribute personally towards road safety by striving to become skilful, economical and responsible.

Recently a comparative test was made by an august motoring body. It consisted of asking two competition drivers of considerable experience to drive two similar cars from Manchester to Land's End via Birmingham. The drivers had instructions which said that car A was to reach its destination as soon as possible without breaking the law; car B was to treat the trip as routine. The result of the test was that car A arrived at Land's End a bare 41 minutes before car B, but had used 3.4 gallons more petrol and the driver confessed to no less than seven potentially hazardous 'incidents'. In contrast, car B, having used far less fuel, arrived with its driver in a relaxed state after an incident-free drive. The moral is perfectly obvious.

The aggressive or boorishly rude person is perhaps even more of a menace on the road than the one who permits the competitive spirit to influence his driving. Unfortunately one thing generally leads to the other, and they are the prime causes of collisions. Remember passengers. A driver who causes them uneasiness or fright is both bad mannered and a rotten driver. Panic is infectious, so try not to start it.

An advanced driver is always considerate of his passengers and polite to other road users of all categories.

Many people ask what the advantage is in passing an advanced driving test or in belonging to an advanced driving organisation. The answers are:

12

(a) you will belong to an exclusive body, all members of which are admitted only on merit;

(b) you can wear the appropriate badge on your car, thus giving you something to live up to;

(c) all the advanced organisations issue appropriate diplomas, certificates, newsletters and so on. They also have special terms with suppliers;

(d) each organisation has its own arrangements with insurers, who offer favourable terms to members who have passed advanced driving tests; [2]

(e) you may have a re-test any time you wish on payment of the appropriate fee. This is particularly useful if you wish to satisfy yourself of your continued competence after a period away from cars, perhaps after an illness or absence from Britain;

(f) husbands and wives may usually pay a combined reduced subscription.

The best and easiest way in which to develop one's observation, and consequently to be able to anticipate the actions of other road users and to time one's own actions accordingly, is to practise the art of the running commentary whilst driving. What is needed here is not merely a catalogue of what a driver is actually doing with the car controls, but a rapid summary of the road picture well ahead, together with an intelligent anticipation of the possible actions of vehicles and pedestrians visible at any one time. Obviously the faster the car is moving the further ahead one's observations must be concentrated. It has been proved by police driving schools and by instructors of advanced driving that a driver who manages to give a satisfactory running commentary whilst negotiating, say, a road through a shopping centre, is a safe and reliable driver. This is also the reason why advanced driving organisations favour the use of the running commentary; it helps their examiners to know what is passing through the candidate's mind. After all, any examiner is only a human being, and the human being who is an expert mind reader is an extremely rare bird. He can only judge the competence of a driver on what he can see and hear that driver observing, planning and doing. Here is an example of commentary driving:

> I am driving a saloon car along a fairly clear road in a built-up area; road curving gently left; speed just over 25 mph; engine temperature normal; car about to pull out of a side road on the left, so watch driver's face — not looking this way — check mirror — cover brake — now he has seen us, so back on accelerator; crossroads ahead is uncontrolled, so ease off and drop to third; glance right, left and right again on approach — OK; accelerate and back to fourth gear. Now there is a lorry parked ahead on our side, so glance underneath for feet of possible jaywalker — OK so proceed normally. The turning between the shops on the right ahead is the one we want, so mirror, signal for right turn, begin slowing as we edge towards centre-line of road, drop to appropriate gear for turn, pay attention to placing car before, during and after the turn, then accelerate. Local knowledge indicates this road leads away from the congested area into the country; check mirror frequently; speed now 30 mph; instruments normal; road narrowing, but we now pass the 'end of restriction' sign; hold present speed because of road surface and width; view over hedge shows the top of a van approaching, so hold well over to the left until we pass. Road widening now, so increase speed to 50 mph, which is legal max here. Two cyclists riding abreast ahead, so gentle blip on horn to warn of our approach — they have now correctly changed to single file; road sign ahead says cattle, so watch for double hazard of animals crossing and maybe mud or other skid risk; arched bridge over road ahead, so watch for approaching traffic using centre of road — clear, so carry on resuming max of 50 mph, but now observe signboard giving name of village ahead, so ease off gradually and

14

enter built-up area at 30 mph. Must be market day — fairly busy — road winds through shopping centre of village; watch for reflections of approaching or emerging traffic in shop windows, and also notice groups of pedestrians chatting on pavements; one might suddenly break away and try to cross without first checking, so ease right down to about 15 mph; school sign ahead, so watch both sides of road carefully — yes, there is a boy running along the pavement on the other side; he'll probably cross in a hurry any moment — there he goes, but our speed was slow enough to allow him over safely.

The above looks easy, and *is* in fact easy, provided you have practised it often enough. At first you will tend to be talking about what has already happened; you will also feel self-conscious — particularly if there is anyone else in the car with you. Never mind, if you persevere you will soon become proficient, and be able to forecast what is about to take place well ahead, as opposed to what is actually taking place just in front of the car. Perseverance at the running commentary technique will, you will soon find, prove very rewarding indeed because it will assist greatly in developing the advance observation upon which your subconscious mind will be able to act. It is this which deals with the mechanical side of driving, such as steering, gear-changing, speed adjustment and so on. What you are actually doing whilst exercising the running commentary is to train the conscious portion of your mind in the fields of observation and planning.

There is another hint well worth knowing for those who are seeking to become really good drivers, and who feel that they could benefit from it. When you are driving, with your wife or a friend in the passenger seat, ask them occasionally to quiz you on the last road sign which you passed, or perhaps shoot an unexpected question at you — for example the colour of the car behind. Try to refrain from checking the mirror before answering. If you can't answer without this help it obviously means your observation is not yet all it could be.

One of the greatest driving faults is indecision, and this is immediately revealed when one begins to practise commentary driving. You perhaps may remember being a learner driver when you often failed to take advantage of quite large traffic gaps and hesitated to emerge from side roads until you considered the expanse of empty road sufficiently inviting. Think back, you will see that you now take advantage of gaps you would have shuddered at the mere thought of attempting then. This in itself should prove to you that practice makes perfect where driving is concerned.

A Green Paper containing a proposed new *Highway Code* was published by the Department of the Environment in January 1975. It has been considered by both Houses of Parliament and many interested organisations are being consulted about the suggested alterations to the present edition, published in February 1969. When the remarks from all concerned have been carefully considered the new version will be submitted to each house for final approval.

The new changes mostly provide for actual changes in motoring laws and driving procedures which have been introduced during recent years which experienced drivers will already know about. Some of them relate to the zig-zag markings at the approach to zebra crossings, the fog code, introduced by Mr John Peyton as Minister for Transport Industries, bus lanes, emergency signals on motorways, railway level crossings and unlit parking at night.

As the 1969 version was under consideration for a very considerable time before being brought into force, no indication can be given as to when the new one is likely to emerge from the press.

THE ADVANCED DRIVING TEST

Basically the actual test is the same, regardless of the

organisation under whose auspices it is held. Naturally there exist some slight differences, but these are too insignificant to matter very much to a competent driver. The most noticeable is that the IAM and the LSD both tend to frown on the practice of 'crossing hands' on the steering wheel, while NADA take a rather more modern and realistic view, in that they take into consideration the actual circumstances in which the candidate found it necessary to 'cross hands'. After all, rally drivers, who are among the most expert in the world, do this, so why not the advanced driver, who may be neither a professional nor a sporting type.

The notification of appointment for the test will give the time and place where you should await the examiner. It is advisable to arrive a few minutes early and park in such a position that the car and numberplate are easily visible from the road, so that he can locate you without delay. He works to a strict timetable and will therefore appreciate such courtesies. Having introduced himself, the examiner will have a discreet look around the car, noting general condition, clean windows, no clutter on the floor and so on and while doing so will talk to you for a few minutes before commencing the actual test. The purpose of this little chat is to tell you exactly how he expects you to drive. Pay particular attention at this stage and, once you move off, bear his instructions in mind the whole time. Some examiners will tell you a running commentary is unnecessary, but stress that you may give one if you feel inclined — accept the invitation, for it helps him to assess your mental processes whilst at the wheel. Here are a few notes of the main points for which they watch:

1 check for safety *every* time you start the engine and/or move away from the kerb. There is no need to signal provided you have done this and are satisfied that it is safe to move off;

2 frequent use of rear-view mirror — especially at the times mentioned in the *Highway Code*, and most particularly before any alteration of course or speed;

17

3 before any alteration of course, mirror, signals (and brakes) should be used *in that order*;

4 always show courtesy to other road users;

5 prove to the examiner that your observation and anticipation is of a high order.

6 always use gentle acceleration, smooth and progressive braking, correct speed on bends and corners;

7 be in the correct lane and gear for the speed that the car may be doing at any given time — especially when approaching junctions;

8 although less attention is now paid to them, because the DoT have accepted that in modern vehicles most drivers prefer to use indicators, your examiner will appreciate it if you occasionally wind down the window and give arm signals. This enables him to assess several points, i.e. the fact that you can control the vehicle whilst doing something else, and your style of giving clear unambiguous signals; also, of course, whether you have chosen to signal in sufficient time to assist following traffic;

9 maintain a safe distance between your vehicle and the one in front;

10 allow a safe clearance when passing cyclists, pedestrians and animals.

As mentioned elsewhere, there will be no trick questions and you will not be asked to carry out any manoeuvre of an extraordinary nature. In addition to turning the car around in the road, the examiner may ask you to reverse into a limited opening either to the left or the right — perhaps both. He will also ask you to bring the car to rest at a precise spot at the end of each reverse. He may also ask for a straight reverse over a given distance keeping the car parallel to the kerb, and perhaps (but not always) to reverse into a space between two cars already parked parallel to the kerb.

Should your car not be fitted with synchromesh on first gear, he will ask you to slow to a speed not below about 5 mph and

18

engage first gear. The technique for this is described elsewhere (see page 73).

Great attention is paid by all examiners to alertness and observation, and you will certainly be asked, perhaps more than once, questions which are designed to reveal just where your eyes have been during the past few moments. Typical questions are about what road signs you may have passed within the last quarter of a mile or so, the type of road junction you have just negotiated (ie was it staggered, controlled or uncontrolled, road surface etc?). Many examiners also ask what at first glance seems to be a rather stupid-sounding question: 'What do you see ahead?' Instead of giving him a pitying look, strive to see just what he really means. Look as far ahead as you possibly can—does the road wind; is there a hedge or low wall over which you can see an obstruction well ahead round the next bend; is there a specimen of that lovely road sign 'concealed level crossing' showing its cross-arms over a hedge ahead? There are, when you come to think about it, many reasons why he could ask such an apparently idiotic question.

On conclusion of the road section of the test, your examiner will ask you to pull in at as safe a spot as you can find. He will then ask a few more questions designed to test your general knowledge as an advanced driver. Make sure you are absolutely familiar with all parts of the *Highway Code*, including the small print, and such advice as you will have read there and elsewhere concerning car maintenance, tyre care and simple motoring jurisprudence. In particular, know the data concerning your own car—what are the recommended tyre pressures; how many gallons does your tank hold; how much does she do to the gallon; what is her width; length; kerb weight; what do you know about towing (if the car is fitted with towing gear), and so on.

On completion of this little third degree, the examiner will probably point out one or more points on which he considers you should concentrate more in order to improve your driving. In any case he will tell you at the end of the session whether you have passed or failed the test, and indicate that you will, in due course, receive an official notification from head office.

In the case of the IAM, you will be sent a small membership card, renewable each year, later followed by a diploma.

The LSD and NADA both provide a written report on your driving, subdivided under such headings as steering, acceleration, braking, cornering, reversing — to the left, the right, parking, use of gears, courtesy to others, and so on. On these you will be able to see the actual marks awarded by the examiner under each heading, which should prove invaluable to you on future occasions. Both of these organisations also provide a small annual membership card as well as the usual diploma.

All the organisations allow members, on passing their tests, to show the appropriate badge on the car, for which a small fee is charged, and all of them discourage the practice of displaying the badge when the car is driven by someone who is not a member.

Anybody in possession of a full driving licence may take these tests, and all organisations encourage members to take occasional re-tests in order to assess continued ability and competence. There is no compulsion about this, except in the case of the League of Safe Drivers (see chapter 7), they only advise it, for serious illness or absence from the road for any appreciable time can result in a variation of driving capabilities more than one realises.

Having passed the test you have chosen, ask the examiner if there is any insurance company which recognises this particular test. He may supply the name of one. This is your cue to ask him to take up with his head office the matter of obtaining recognition from all companies. Don't just leave it at that, though. Write to your MP and ask him to do the same.*

*See Note 2 at end of book.

20

CHAPTER TWO

Improving Your Technique

British roads and, more particularly, country lanes are congenitally incapable of maintaining a straight course for any appreciable distance. Driving in the lanes is much more interesting and rewarding than ploughing along for hours in the wake of other traffic. It is also much more useful from the point of view of bettering one's driving techniques. Unfortunately in our charming country lanes, where even two Minis would have difficulty in passing safely, some people drive as though there could not possibly be the slightest likelihood of any traffic coming in the opposite direction.

It is a fact that the longer one drives, the more nonchalant one is likely to become and, as a result, one gradually develops an individual technique. All too often this includes late braking, failure to observe road signs, inattention to other drivers, their positioning and signals, and last, but not least, the habit of coasting instead of actually driving. All of which may, and probably will, prove fatal some day.

The short answer to all this is self-discipline all the time one is behind the wheel. This fact is inescapable—a moment's carelessless could cost your own life or that of another, perhaps a child.

Cultivate smooth driving and pay careful attention to road and traffic conditions. Always maintain a correct 'hangback' position behind other vehicles. Younger drivers will have speedier reactions than their elders, and may therefore be able to cope with situations which could prove disastrous to older drivers, but, until experience has been gained, it pays to observe the advice contained in the *Highway Code*, ie keep a distance of at least one yard per mile per hour between you and the vehicle ahead. This is, of course, assuming ideal conditions. One factor could be absent on any one occasion, for instance road conditions might have deteriorated, or you might be nearing the end of a long journey and fairly tired, or (one hesitates to suggest) your tyres may be nearing the end of their useful or legal life. In such cases, of course, a prudent driver will increase the hangback position to perhaps double in order to allow for unforeseen braking on the part of the car in front. Despite constant emphatic warnings from the police and all motoring organisations, the single factor responsible for repeated multiple crashes on motorways is failure to observe this precept concerning hangback. It stands to reason that when conditions deteriorate a vehicle will be unable to stop safely in the same distance which was possible in ideal conditions, but the majority of drivers persistently fail to adjust their speed and distance accordingly. This is probably one of the greatest single causes of accidents, and you, as an aspiring master driver, must always bear it in mind.

Car positioning on corners and bends is important. A fruitful source of failure on all types of driving test, carelessly negotiated corners are not only a sign of a thoughtless driver, but positively dangerous to other road users.

Refresh your memory of the *Highway Code*, upon which *all* tests, elementary and advanced, are based; your bookseller will obtain the latest edition for you. Naturally, you should already be familiar with it, including the small print, but to make sure you are on the correct road to driving faultlessly, read it meticulously and check your own driving against its teachings.

In normal driving, always position the car correctly before overtaking and check for safety both ahead and astern before initiating the manoeuvre. The *Highway Code* devotes several sections to this particular action—an indication of its importance. Make sure you know the circumstances in which it is actually dangerous to overtake.

Speed of approach to junctions and crossroads is again something which many drivers don't seem to bother too much about.

A good driver never cuts in on other traffic, never overtakes at a dangerous time or place, never allows his car to become sandwiched between others and never cuts corners or takes them too wide.

In order to satisfy yourself of your own peripheral vision, either have it checked, or make yourself a giant protractor out of cardboard and hold it horizontally before your eyes. Then

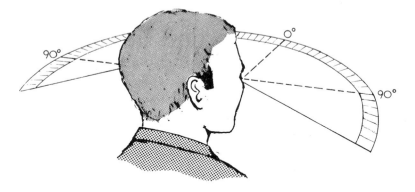

Figure 1   Checking peripheral vision

get a friend to stand just behind you. Ask him to lift a hand and gradually advance it along the curved edge of the protractor, first on one side, and then the other. This will give a rough but practical guide of your normal arc of vision. The nearer it is to 180 degrees, the better.

Good road planning today provides for long straight stretches or gentle curves affording good forward vision, but increased speed means observation distance must also be increased if you are not to be caught off guard.

Although motorways completely eliminate interruption from cross traffic, entering vehicles, pedestrians, learners and so on, one must always realise that the accepted high speeds necessitate a completely different code of behaviour. Frequent consultation of facia gauges is important; petrol, oil pressure, engine temperature, charging rate and so on. Failure to watch such apparently minor but very important tell-tale signs has been the cause of much inconvenience and unnecessary expense for people who have experienced engine failure as a result. Restaurants, garages and filling stations, although few in number, are strategically sited, and if you notice anything amiss, then it should be possible to drive gently on to the next one — provided you have noticed the trouble in time. Prevention is not only better, but also usually much cheaper than cure. After all, a sudden rise in water temperature may only mean a slipping or broken fanbelt; taking things steadily to the next service station is the obvious solution.

Of course it is essential that brakes, tyres, steering, lights and other items are in good condition, but as a budding master driver you will naturally attend to all those things as a matter of routine.

The faster one drives, the more necessary becomes frequent use of the rear-view mirror.

Motorways, being based on the dual carriageway system, are the safest type of road when intelligently used, but probably the most dangerous when used by inexperienced or irresponsible drivers. For this reason it is a good idea to omit them from one's itinerary should conditions be much below normal, for instance fog, blinding snowstorms and so on.

These are the conditions in which multiple collisions proliferate. No matter how good a driver you may be, you will still be unable to see through thick fog or a blizzard, and it is fatally easy to run into a pile of mangled vehicles and bodies hidden by weather conditions. In such situations sanity spells survival.

It is an accepted fact that the most lethal type of road is the three-lane one. Cars approach at high speeds and, with even a blanket speed limit of 50 mph, a collision *could* mean an impact speed of 100 mph. Dusk is the worst time on most roads, but on the three-lane type it pays to be at the peak of alertness, especially at holiday times.

Drivers have been heard to boast that in an emergency they can stop within the car's length, but the finest driver in the world in the best car in the world could do no such thing. The distances mentioned in the *Highway Code* are not there in order to scare learners into solemn and sedate behaviour, they are fairly realistic, and from them it can be seen that stopping depends mainly upon two things:

1 the driver's reaction time;
2 the speed of the car when the brakes are applied.

The average person has a reaction time of something like .75 second under ideal conditions, but many are very much slower, stretching to more than two seconds. It follows, therefore, that stopping distances will vary with individual drivers.

Braking distances depend, in turn, upon several things — the type and efficiency of the car's braking system, the braking force available at the driver's foot, and so on. It can be shown that braking distance increases roughly as the square of the speed of the car between 20 and 50 mph. At higher speeds the distance increases even more rapidly.

Personal reaction times can be improved by always being alert, by becoming completely familiar with the car and its performance, and paying careful attention to the traffic conditions at all times in order to recognise a potential collision situation as early as possible.

The question of braking brings up the point that the entire control of a moving car is dependent upon the grip which four small areas of tyre have upon the road. This grip is dependent upon friction, enabling the car to start, stop and maintain traction, as well as to be steered. If friction is reduced, driver control is also reduced. It follows that the higher the coefficient of friction, the better the control — this is the case with good tyres and a dry road. Friction is a basic fact of nature, and a driver who understands and respects its limitations will have a high degree of car control. For this reason, practice upon a skidpan is to be strongly recommended if it can possibly be arranged.

All this is closely tied up with the successful negotiation of curves at speed. A car moving in a straight line tends to maintain that line, but, if its direction is altered, centrifugal force will try to pull it back at a tangent to the curve being negotiated. If the road surface on the curve is slippery there will be a corresponding reduction of friction between tyres and road. Under such conditions accurate steering becomes impossible. How serious the result of this will be can depend upon:

1 the speed of the car;
2 the camber of the road;
3 the sharpness of the curve;
4 road conditions (dry, wet, icy, etc);
5 the state of the tyres (depth of tread and tread pattern);
6 the skill of the driver in taking corrective action.

Of these, the car's speed is the most important and is also the one over which the driver has the most control.

As in other situations, good forward observation will be vital, since it enables the driver to assess the acuteness of the bend and to adjust the speed of the car accordingly. The negotiation of curves highlights good or bad driving habits.

Good drivers begin to slow before entering a bend, not when they are actually in it, and the good driver also knows that a car is more controllable in a curve when the engine is pulling. When either on the overrun, or braking, there is some loss of control. It is therefore preferable to enter any curve at such a speed that it may be negotiated under slight acceleration. A driver who is seen to apply his brakes in a bend is to be avoided, since this is a blatant sign of lack of skill.

Other things which have an adverse effect on friction are wet leaves, snow and ice, gravel, rain after a long spell of sunshine, and oil or grease on the road. Once again observation and sensible anticipation will assist in deciding whether the surface is good enough for firm braking. If it is smooth and well worn it will present a glazed appearance, and very likely lack friction; on the other hand, if it has a dull, matt appearance it may reasonably be assumed to be a relatively safe surface.

Everyday driving in company with other vehicles today requires, more than ever, a high degree of alertness to enable you to keep out of the other man's accident. In driving, as in games, there is fair play and foul, and the good driver is the one who not only sticks to the rules but does so in a sporting manner. Driving courtesy goes far beyond the bare observance of rules and regulations. The good driver yields right-of-way, even at times when it may be legally his, in various circumstances — say, for instance, that he sees another vehicle in a difficult traffic situation, or obviously having been waiting to emerge from a side road for some time. Other drivers may disregard the unfortunate one's predicament, but not our master driver; he will make his 'I intend to slow down or stop' signal for the benefit of following traffic and let the waiting car emerge safely.

Good driving is also defensive driving, which takes no advantage of either mistakes or lack of skill in others. Streets and highways are public property, and the driver who behaves badly upon them is rightly condemned by legal process. There

27

are a great many ways in which good road manners may be displayed, but the following are some of the best examples:

1 dip headlights to oncoming cars at night;

2 use dipped headlights when driving behind others;

3 follow at a safe distance;

4 drive at such a speed that you can stop safely within the distance you can see to be clear;

5 maintain correct lane discipline;

6 make full use of driving mirrors;

7 give early and clear signals;

8 give pedestrians and cyclists adequate clearance;

9 make certain that your vehicle is, at all times, in perfect condition.

A good driver usually, but not necessarily, maintains a good average speed. He does this by correctly reading and assessing the road ahead and driving in such a manner that the minimum of gear-changing, braking and consequent acceleration is necessary.

Reference to Fig 2 will show that one's position on the road

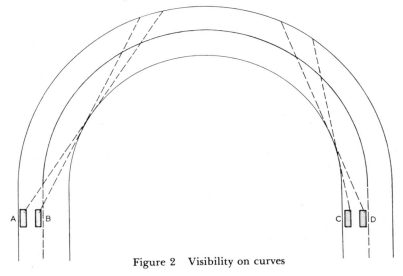

Figure 2   Visibility on curves

has a direct bearing on adjustment of speed. The driver of car A, negotiating a right-hand curve and keeping well to his left, can obviously see much further than the driver of car B on the same curve, and can therefore feel safe to drive at a higher speed. Similarly, the driver of car C, entering a left-hand curve, is unable to see as far as the driver of car D, who is holding his vehicle out towards the centre line of the road. To summarise: entering a right-hand curve, keep well to the left; entering a left-hand curve, hold out towards the centre line for maximum visibility — provided all is safe.

This advice is contradicted by the DoT's driving manual, and by the *Highway Code*, so who is right?

Here is an anomaly, but in their own way both the DoT and the motoring pundits are correct. The advanced driving organisations, the police, and instructors of advanced techniques are advising those who are already experienced drivers, but the DoT has to lay down rules without equivocation or reservation for 20 or 30 million licence holders. The manual *Driving*, in my view, considerably overstresses the point by saying 'keep well to the left' which could be construed as meaning a position much closer to the nearside than normal, thus restricting a driver's view ahead into a left-hand corner or bend. *Driving* continues the argument by asking 'What should I do if the last vehicle to take the bend has broken down just out of sight around the corner?' The answer lies in the advice given above, for by positioning too much to the left you would obviously see the broken-down vehicle much too late to take successful evasive action. The broken-down vehicle will also serve to block the view ahead of it very effectively, bearing in mind that a large number of drivers, faced with such a situation, would not brake, but steer outwards in order to avoid the obvious obstacle ahead, thus making confusion worse. Another point here is that, since any pedestrians would be walking towards oncoming traffic, they, too, would be endangered by vehicles hugging the left-hand side of the road—more so if there were no footpath.

The correct answer in this, as in all other cases of contention, is to drive according to the circumstances. There is a time and place for both methods, and more often than not for a compromise between the two. Commonsense should dictate technique wherever doubt exists.

The broken-down vehicle in the case above should, of course, have been using hazard warning indicators and/or a reflective triangle positioned sufficiently before the bend for an oncoming driver to receive adequate warning, but not all vehicles carry them, although it is against the law not to do so on the continent; an example we could well emulate.

Constant reference is made in the motoring press to the evident need for further training for newly qualified drivers, despite which it would appear that only a mere 2 per cent of all motorists consider this worthwhile, according to figures published by the Royal Society for the Prevention of Accidents. For the 'accident-prone' under twenty-four age group this attitude is reflected in their 'nearly one-third' contribution to the annual fatal and serious accident figures. The three main advanced driving organisations confirm this picture. IAM reports, for example, claim that some 78 per cent of their failures are due to a combination of incorrect assessment, poor safety margins and unsystematic procedure at hazards and in cornering. Reference to the figures given in Chapter Six, concerning failure rates of candidates for advanced driving tests, will make the position even clearer. The horrifying thing is that these are candidates for IAM membership who obviously consider themselves good drivers or they wouldn't apply for the test. Their failure rate proves otherwise. What then of the novices?

Certainly NADA, the IAM and the League of Safe Drivers are doing a splendid job, as are very many driving schools throughout the country. Seemingly, though, nothing can convince most drivers that a relatively modest cash outlay would, in the long run, save very much bigger ones for damage, injury resulting in medical treatment, and funerals. The *Motoring Guardian* reports that the BSM Advanced Course has been taken by only 1,600 people in eleven years, out of whom roughly 400 failed to qualify. The fact that we have something like thirty-odd million drivers on the roads today, when compared with these figures, makes one think rather deeply.

In 1959 the RAC introduced what they called a 'Junior Driver Course'. This aimed to reduce the risk of an accident occurring during the relatively dangerous period between passing the driving test of the DoT and the time when some experience alone on the road had been acquired. In 1968 the course was revised to meet current needs, and has been brought up to date regularly to correspond with changing traffic conditions and legal requirements. As a result it may now be taken in two parts, the first seeking to educate youth, preferably starting whilst still at school, thus allowing young people to benefit from the 'pre-driver training' given in part I of the course. It is offered through the large network of RAC registered instructors throughout Britain, and full particulars may be obtained from the Royal Automobile Club Junior Training Scheme, 83-85 Pall Mall, London SW1.

One of the most valuable forms of practice is that of parking the car between others close to the kerb. It also has the advantage that it may be practised almost anywhere so long as there is an adequate space between two cars already parked. Many people just drive headlong into the first vacant space they see, leaving the stern of the vehicle protruding dangerously into the road, causing a hazard for others. Quite apart from endangering your own car, a police patrol would be quite justified in booking you for causing a dangerous obstruction. It is not too difficult to drive just past the car ahead of the space you have selected (having first checked for safety and signalled your intentions to slow down and stop),

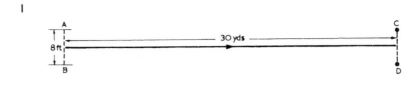

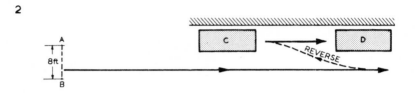

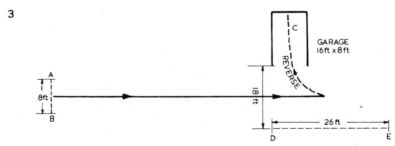

Figure 3   Exercises to improve car handling. These exercises are based upon the tests usually set in the annual L Driver of the Year Competition run by the Royal Automobile Club, and are reproduced here with their kind permission

1   Start with front wheels on AB and from driving seat instruct Marshal to place markers C and D in order that car will pass between them with minimum of side clearance. Then drive forward and stop with widest part of car on line CD.

Marking

Deduct: 3 points per inch or part of in excess of 6 inches total clearance (sum of two sides). 50 points for touching either or both markers C and D. Penalty for non-completion, 100 points.

2 Start with front wheels on AB, drive forward then reverse to park, with both nearside wheels within 12 inches of kerb between vehicles C and D. From AB five movements are permitted, those in excess of three incurring penalty.

Marking

Deduct: 1 point for each inch or part of in excess of 12 inches from kerb to tyre, (a) at front; (b) at rear; 50 points each time for touching vehicle C and 50 points each time for touching vehicle D; 10 points each time for touching kerb; 10 points for each movement in excess of three.

Penalty for non-completion, 170 points.

3 Start with front wheels on AB, drive forward left of DE and reverse into garage C. Once reversing starts, driving forward will result in loss of marks.

Marking

Deduct: 100 points for touching rear wall, 5 points for each inch or part over 6 inches from rear wall, 50 points each time for touching either side wall, 10 points for each movement forward after first reverse, 50 points each time a wheel touches line DE.

Penalty for non-completion, 250 points.

then reverse very slowly until your nearside rear wing comes level with the offside wing of the car behind which you intend to park. Now steer left to aim the stern of your vehicle at the kerb roughly midway between the two cars ahead and astern of your intended parking spot. Continue slowly backwards, transferring your attention to the nearside front wing of your own car. As it starts to clear the stern of the car ahead of you swing the wheel over sharply to the right, thus bringing your own car sharply inwards. Correct judgement will result in very neat parking indeed, and will have the advantage that your front wheels will already be on right lock when you come to drive out. Novices are not generally taught to carry out this relatively simple manoeuvre, although they should be, for it is excellent practice in the development of judgement, and makes one familiar with the length and width of one's car.

The sight of a car correctly reversed into a suburban driveway is, in many districts, comparatively rare, but it is by far the safest way to park the car outside your house. This should be particularly so if there is a wall or hedge at the front of your house likely to cause blind spots.

Make use of anything which can be construed as practice in car handling. Even the white line across the road at traffic lights can be used as a marker (when you are first in the queue). The ideal, and therefore correct, place to bring the car to rest is with the front bumper vertically above the white line. Try it first at a place where you can make a mark, then, after bringing the car to rest where you think is the correct position, get out and have a look. You may be surprised. The trick is to draw a chalk line in the correct position relative to the front bumper, and extend it a couple of feet to the offside of the car, so that when you sit in the driving seat you will be able to see where the line apparently falls in relation to the offside, or some portion of it. With very little practice you will soon be able to place the car accurately every time.

There are many such exercises which you can devise for yourself with the aid of a few pieces of tape and some old cardboard boxes. These form the basis of several competitive driving tests.

One which you can try on a deserted airfield, or some similar piece of wasteland, is to set up six poles or wands in a straight line, at intervals equal to one-and-a-half car-lengths between each. Now, with the car in line with the file of rods, drive forward, weaving in and out between alternate poles, finishing approximately in line with, and well beyond, the last pole. Now reverse, going from lock to lock as you weave backwards through them, finishing clear of, and in line with, the last one (which was the first one). This exercise used to form part of the RAC L Driver of the Year competition and par for the course was two minutes. Think that is too generous? Well have a try.

Far from being pointless, the few simple exercises suggested here will, if practised fairly frequently, result in your becoming very adept at car handling in confined and difficult places—one of the hallmarks of a good and competent driver.

A few more exercises will suggest themselves to you.

Those described are actually used, not only in the L Driver of the Year event, but also in quite a number of special tests at the end of club rallies. Local authorities are also fond of organising what they gaily refer to as 'safety rallies', so even if you don't decide to go in for the more hectic forms of motor sport, why not have a go at your local safety rally? No competition licence is required for participants, and sometimes the prizes are worthwhile, in addition to benefits on the social side.

Road Signs. There are, as every thinking driver will have observed, instances of misplaced and/or technically incorrect road signs in various localities, and where these are seen it is worthwhile reporting them to the district office of the motoring organisation to which you belong. It is one of the things for which they are continually on the look-out, and they will be grateful for the opinions of individual drivers.

Headlamp Signals. These have no meaning according to the *Highway Code* and, in fact, can, if misinterpreted, be a direct cause of accidents. There have been many 'unofficial' interpretations placed upon them from time to time, such as a short flash signifying 'it is safe for you to proceed now', or a long one meaning 'I intend to come through'. It all depends upon what you mean by long or short. The best thing is not to rely upon such signals at all, but to decide for yourself just how safe or otherwise it is to proceed under certain circumstances, for you are solely responsible for the safety of your vehicle. A possible exception might be when being overtaken by a long vehicle, or by a vehicle towing another, to let the driver know when it is safe to pull back into his lane, for he may not always be able to see the car he has just overtaken properly, in relation to his own rear end. In any case this is merely an extension of the *Highway Code* meaning of 'I am here'.

Arm Signals. There is an increasing tendency for these to be omitted, and for drivers to rely almost entirely upon traffic indicators. This is all very well as far as it goes, but I would venture to suggest that there are two instances when the arm signal meaning 'I intend to slow down or stop' could, with advantage, replace indicator signals:

1 if the intention is to stop alongside the kerb some little (but safe) distance before a side turning on the left. In this case a direction indicator signal could mislead a following driver into believing that the vehicle ahead of him is about to turn left at the junction;

2 in the event of any unscheduled, and therefore unexpected, stop in a stream of traffic. The arm signal, made *before* touching the brake pedal and actuating the 'stop' lights of the car will give following traffic that few seconds extra warning which may, and should, eliminate the possibility of a rear-end collision.

CHAPTER THREE

Car Sympathy

Since a car is a relatively complicated piece of mechanism, it stands to reason that unless it is treated properly it will soon begin to give its owner trouble. It will therefore pay him handsomely to make a habit of cultivating that indefinable 'something' which experienced drivers call 'car sympathy'. Some very obvious examples of this are gentle acceleration, early and smooth braking, avoidance of jerky steering, gear-changing, swerving on corners, and so on. In fact practically anything which would be likely to cause more rapid wear than that normally experienced in everyday use, and this applies to every part of the car.

Driving a car entails two separate and distinct skills, ie car control, a purely manual skill, and roadcraft, more of a mental discipline. The latter has been dealt with in the earlier chapters, since most people consider it to be the be-all and end-all of advanced driving. There is much more to it than that, however. It is not the slightest use being the best exponent of roadcraft in the district if your car handling leaves shreds of metal and rubber all over the road. Even if that is an exaggeration, the end result comes to the same thing — an accident caused by vehicle failure — and surely that is not the mark of a master driver!

Here, then, are a few points which, if religiously observed, will certainly extend the life of your car and at the same time reduce your maintenance and repair bills:

1 avoid excessive use of the choke when starting from cold; never permit the engine to idle, but drive off immediately, for this in itself will minimise engine wear. Neat petrol washes oil down from the cylinder walls;

2 even during tricky manoeuvres in confined places, try to slip the clutch as little as possible, and when you do so do not race the engine, for that burns clutch linings. Modern engines are designed with much lighter clutch plates than those of yore, and high revving could even crack the pressure plate;

3 for the same reason, enthusiastic acceleration when moving away from a stationary position is to be avoided. It also wastes fuel, wears tyres badly and ruins the suspension;

4 the designer provided a first gear for your car. If he had wished to save money on manufacturing costs he could have eliminated it, but he chose not to do so. He isn't a fool, or he wouldn't hold his job. Therefore, use the gear he provided for moving off from rest. If you bypass first gear your clutch will be rapidly ruined. So will the big ends and all sorts of other things;

5 restrain your enthusiasm for acceleration until the engine has warmed to a normal working temperature — watch those dials;

6 vicious cornering means a high expenditure in tyres and can also induce skids when the weather deteriorates ever so slightly — sometimes even on dry roads;

7 treat your windscreen as if it were a delicate skin. It is, in a way. You wouldn't wipe your eyes with sandpaper, so why use the wipers on a dry screen, where minute particles of dust will turn them into most efficient abrasives within the first couple of sweeps. Wet the screen thoroughly before switching them on. Examine the blades regularly; they should be replaced (on a car which is regularly used) at the start of every winter;

8 overloading the engine will soon put paid to bushes, bearings and journals — in fact every moving part which bears a load. By overloading or 'slogging' the engine, repair bills may be increased out of all proportion to the car's mileage;

9 another way to ruin the clutch quickly is to use the pedal as a footrest — but only beginners do that, don't they?;

10 slowing early for corners, obstacles, traffic lights and so on is not only ɔod practice from a roadcraft point of view, it also means lighter braking pressures, and consequent savings on replacement brake linings and tyres. There is also the point that late braking, which involves greater pressures, can also cause skids and collisions;

11 use a tyre blackening paint. It will have the effect of showing up immediately on the tyre itself any spot at which you have touched the kerb. Not only will it enhance the appearance of your car, but it will serve as a deterrent to kerbing your tyres. It also provides an indication as to where you should inspect your tyres most meticulously;

12 handbrake turns are useful things to know about, but on no account try to use them in normal roadwork or you will probably scare half the population in sight. Always apply the handbrake *after* the car stops, because it works only on the rear wheels, and could therefore cause a skid. In any case it will certainly cause excessive wear. Also make a habit of always squeezing the little button on the end of the handle, both when applying and releasing the lever. Ignoring it not only makes an unnecessary scrunching noise, but causes the ratchet to wear rapidly and maybe unevenly. A bad habit here could, one day, land you in serious trouble should the car run away on a hill whilst unoccupied;

13 the steering gear is one of the most important assemblies on a car, so treat it with a great deal of respect. Never turn the wheel when the car is stationary. If you have them jacked up and wish to turn the front wheels from side to side for

servicing, do so very gently, especially near the ends of either lock, in order to avoid strain on components;

14 *any* unusual noise can be, and probably is, an early warning of trouble, which might prove serious. Treat any squeak, rattle, bang or crunch as serious until you have proved otherwise — it may prove only to be something loose, worn or slightly out of adjustment, but if neglected this could cause an accident.

The term 'car sympathy' goes much further than merely driving it carefully. Attention to the state of the bodywork is important, for, although with the range of chemicals and sprays now available it is relatively easy to do quite a bit of touching up, and even minor first-aid jobs to the paintwork, the large-scale repair of damaged panels is best left to the expert. You as an experienced driver will, of course, be unlikely to cause appreciable damage to your own car or others, but it is a sad fact that bumpers, wings and so on are still likely to suffer from damage sustained in car parks when you are not there to see.

If you do find an odd, small dent, don't attempt to eliminate it by any kind of amateur panel beating; this kind of thing is a skilled job. It is much better to fill minor dents or scratches, rub down the area concerned with very smooth (grade 400) 'wet or dry' paper until flush with the surrounding coachwork, then spray with one of the matching aerosols which are on the market. The time and effort you spend in obtaining a really smooth finish when rubbing down will be rewarded by the excellent gloss resulting when the paint is applied. Before spraying, remove all traces of wax polish with white spirit unless the polish contains silicones, in which case more drastic treatment is required such as the use of a 'cutting' compound like some of the old-fashioned metal polishes. Remember that ageing causes paint to change colour, so it is really better to spray a whole panel than a small area. When actually using the aerosol, try to keep the central area wet and the outer edges somewhat dryer and lighter. After spraying, leave the work for a day or so, then use the cutting compound lightly again to remove the surface dryness of the spray, and finish off with your usual polish.

In bad weather local authorities spread grit and salt on roads in order to minimise skidding and wheelspin. This is all very well at the time, but if you have to drive in such conditions, then make very sure that you hose down the underside of the car with fresh water as soon afterwards as is practicable, for nothing attacks the underside of a car faster than salt. This advice applies also to those holidaymakers who run their vehicles close to the sea. A whitish deposit is always a warning sign, and should be heeded immediately. Luckily the upperwork of the vehicle suffers least in these conditions because a shower of fresh rainwater usually clears away the worst of the enemy, but unfortunately 'out of sight, out of mind' applies to the underparts. Make sure you don't forget them or drastic things will soon begin to happen to the floor, the suspension, the petrol tank, the brake cables and other bits and pieces — all expensive to replace or rectify.

Occasionally inspect the underseal and renew where necessary after first scraping away a portion of the surrounding area and rubbing it down with a wire brush. Prevention of rust underneath a car is far and away much better than cure. There are several proprietary rust removers, all of which seem to work pretty well, but, if you have to use one, do read the directions carefully and follow them religiously; some have to be washed off, while others may be painted over. In any case it is always best to get rid of the surface rust before commencing the alchemy business. For this, use that wire brush freely.

Overestimation of the capabilities of one's vehicle probably causes more damage to engines owned by novices than to those driven by experienced drivers, so make sure when you load up more than usual, or perhaps tow a van or boat, that the extra burden is well within the capacity of the car.

41

INSURANCE WHEN TOWING

There is nothing in the customary private car policy as issued by most of the big insurance companies which specifically excludes towing, and you don't even have to inform your insurers that you intend to do so. As a matter of courtesy, however, and to place it on record that you have actually kept them informed of all that you intend to do, it would be wise to drop them a line if you plan to take a caravan or boat on holiday. The insurance position is similar for boats, caravans and small trailers, ie for the purpose of the Road Traffic Act these, when attached to the towing car, are identified with it. The motorist is therefore covered against third party risks for both, unless there is a specific exclusion in his policy.

Of course, when the boat or caravan is detached from the car it must be covered by a separate policy. A special caravan policy normally includes loss or damage when actually towing without discrimination, but this is not always so with a boat policy. The boat policy is issued by yacht insurers, one type covering small craft up to 16ft, and the other larger craft. The small-craft policy includes loss or damage whilst the craft is being towed on the road, and is useful for those who lay up their craft at home and periodically take it to a launching site. The larger-yacht policy does not include towing risks, although this may be separately arranged. Usually it costs little or nothing extra for craft up to 25ft. For anything larger the insurance company will undoubtedly require a larger premium.

There is, of course, no legal requirement for third-party insurance for boats whilst afloat, although there is an increasing demand from marina and mooring authorities for this cover, in order to protect owners of other craft against a boat dragging, breaking adrift, or catching fire and so causing damage.

Before attempting to tow, it would be wise to make yourself

familiar with all rules and regulations relating to towing, and ensure that your particular car is suitable for your caravan or boat.

CHAPTER FOUR

Economy Driving

Since the sudden panic about the paucity of the nation's fuel reserves during 1973, there has been a great deal of attention paid to economy.

The immediate result of this is that cars giving more mileage to the gallon have become much more popular. However, there are a great number of ways in which economy can be practised, some of which are considered below.

Brakes. It is perfectly logical to begin with these, for even slightly binding or unevenly adjusted brakes can affect the performance of a vehicle to a great extent. Park on a level surface and, with the gears in neutral, try to push the car. If it does not roll freely, or if there is the slightest creaking or rubbing noise, maybe the handbrake is binding; check the cables, slacken them and lubricate where necessary. With the handbrake performing satisfactorily, drive the car for a few miles, using the brakes as sparingly as possible, then try to come to a stop without using them at all. Feel the drums and discs to see if any are running hot. If so attend to it at once.

Tyres. There is much more here to look after than meets the untutored eye. Pressures should be exactly as stated in the owner's handbook; wrongly adjusted pressures can not only

get you into trouble with the law, but can affect the steering of
the car in addition to causing uneven wear on the tyres
themselves. Reference to Fig 4 will help to explain the results

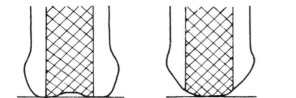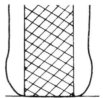

Figure 4   How incorrect tyre pressures can cause uneven wear: *left*, under
inflation causes wear at outer edges of tyre tread; *centre*, over inflation
causes wear in centre of tyre tread; *right*, correct inflation results in even
wear throughout. Quite apart from the legal and/or economical considerations resulting from the above, unless tyre pressures are correct, the steering
and road-holding characteristics of your car will be impaired if pressures are
wrongly adjusted. It is wise to check them daily

of under- or over-inflation, but, in addition, an under-inflated
tyre does not have sufficient air to cushion the road shocks; it
will therefore heat up, and may eventually burst. It also makes
for heavy steering. Over-inflation certainly has a lower rolling
resistance, but the tread is no longer flat on the ground, so it
wears more heavily at the centre. The little extra you may gain
in fuel consumption will be offset by the necessity for an earlier
tyre change.

Lubrication. Probably the heading under which the
uninformed are most likely to do their cheese-paring.
Remember that friction wastes energy. Never skimp on oil-
changes, and always carry them out at the recommended
intervals for your car. The makers know best. A further point
is that *every* time the oil is changed it is good practice to
replace the filter element — it is the filter which keeps your oil
clean and efficient, and they cost, as a rule, well under a
pound.

Whilst attending to oil-changes, do not overlook the

gearbox and back axle (if your car isn't a front-wheel-drive model which has an integral gearbox and no rear axle to be topped up).

Wheel Bearings. These need greasing only at rare intervals — something like 36,000 miles, but if you ever take over a second-hand vehicle, then make sure this point is one of those which will be attended to at an early date. Previous owners may have neglected such things. A faulty wheel bearing is readily detected; it makes a rumbling noise which is most noticeable when going downhill on the overrun, or when cornering with the faulty wheel on the outside of the bend. If you decide to do the job yourself, beg, borrow, or buy a torque wrench, for the hub nut must be accurately tightened to the manufacturers' specification. An over-tight bearing causes excessive fuel consumption and wears rapidly, while a loose one is not to be recommended for obvious reasons.[3]

Prop Shafts and Universal Joints. These units are now usually sealed for the life of the car, but should be checked to make sure no grease is oozing out and that there is no excessive play. If any joint is covered by a fabric or rubber gaiter, ensure that it remains intact.

Steering and Suspension. Attention to these will extend their useful life and retain the car's driving characteristics which were so carefully developed by its maker. It is here that tracking should be checked to ensure even tread wear on the front wheels.

If you go to the bother (and it is worth it) of keeping a record of fuel consumption, you will notice the benefit conferred by regular and meticulous servicing. A 10-15 per cent improvement immediately after a service is quite common, provided the service has been correctly carried out. One of the most important items in this connection is the distributor contact-breaker points, unless of course you have electronic ignition fitted. These points become pitted and eroded owing to the electric spark having to leap across them; also any alteration in the size of the gap between them not only alters the characteristic of the spark itself, but also changes the timing, which is an important factor. It is not quite enough just to reset the gap after cleaning and flattening the surfaces of the points. Ideally, timing should be set and checked by the use of a dwell angle meter and a stroboscopic light at the engine speeds laid down by the manufacturers, in order to make sure that the automatic advance and retard mechanisms are functioning satisfactorily. Having done this, or having had it done for you by an expert at your friendly local garage, the sparking plugs may be attended to. Ensure that the leads are in good condition and not fouled by oil or water. Check the caps for cleanliness and possible fracture. Replace them every 10,000 miles, ensuring that they are the correct type for your engine, but between changes they should be cleaned and their points adjusted regularly. Valve clearance adjustments are usually beyond the private owner, but should be specified for attention when major services are undertaken by your garage. Insufficient clearance prevents the valves from closing completely, the gases will not be correctly contained and the exhaust valves will disintegrate. Over-large clearances do not permit the valves to open fully and impair the efficiency of the engine; also wear on the cam followers will increase, as will engine noise.

Attention to the air cleaner at the carburettor intake should be a matter of course, for one which is bunged up both increases petrol consumption and reduces power. A great deal of abrasive material which adversely affects the engine can enter through this inlet, so change the filter regularly. Having now approached the carburettor, check all linkages including those of the choke and accelerator. Some cars have inherently jerky accelerator cables, and these may be replaced with nylon ones, available from your local shop, but make sure you get the correct type for your make and model. Correct adjustment of the idle-mixture strength necessitates the use of an exhaust gas analyser, so is best entrusted to a qualified mechanic whose speciality is carburettors.

Petrol being sold in two-, three-, four- and five-star grades may confuse some drivers who either plump for the highest grade if they want a lively performance, or the lowest when they are nearing the end of the month. This is a fallacy. There is nothing more or less 'powerful' about the various grades of petrol; five-star contains no more chemical energy than two-star. The higher grade fuel's only advantage lies in its ability to resist what the pundits call 'detonation' — an undesirable tendency for the firing of the mixture to occur as a sharp explosion instead of smoothly. As a general rule, the higher the star grade, or octane rating, the more suitable it is for an engine with a high compression ratio. Even here we can't really generalise, for today we have engines with as high a compression ratio as 9:1 which will function perfectly well on two-star fuel. A quick check that you are using a suitable grade is to accelerate hard at about 25 mph on a level road. If you are able, ignore the protests from the engine and transmission system, but listen carefully for a sharp 'pinking' noise which indicates that a higher grade of fuel should be used.

Oil companies work closely in conjunction with the major car manufacturers to ensure that the lubricants they formulate are as suitable as possible for the engines for which they are intended. For this reason there should be no necessity for the use of additives. Tests carried out by independent bodies such as the AA, RAC and the advanced driving organisations have found none which have significantly improved lubrication. Blending chemical additives and base oils is an exact science, and it is easy to upset the delicate chemical balance of a good oil. Generally speaking, therefore, most additives, although expensive, add nothing to performance, but can have thickening properties which contribute to difficult starting and shorten battery life.

Now that the car has received all the attention due to it, by

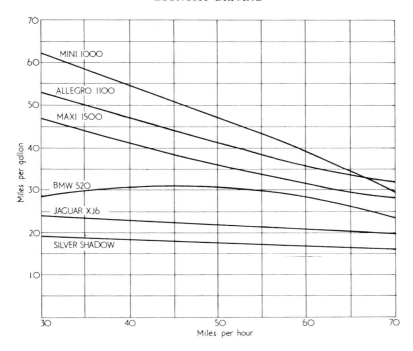

Figure 5   Miles per gallon obtained on typical standard models

far the most effective manner in which you can contribute to economy is to drive more smoothly and gently. Please refer to Fig 5; this shows clearly just how hard driving affects fuel consumption with average cars. Of course, if you can afford to run the more expensive models shown, then economy is not usually your prime consideration anyway. These figures were obtained on long runs, but if you generally use the car for short 'stop-start' runs in town, as, for instance, a doctor on his rounds or a person who has to make a number of local calls at shops or firms, then your petrol bill will bear no relation whatever to these figures. Driving in heavy traffic in town is notoriously wasteful, as is using it for going to and from work, unless 'work' is sufficiently far away to permit the engine to

49

warm up thoroughly and have a nice long gear-change-free run. A person who starts the car and lets it warm up by ticking over in the drive while he finishes breakfast is doing neither his petrol bill nor his engine the slightest bit of good; such a practice wastes fuel, causes cylinder wear and contaminates the oil. Do not start the car until you are ready, and then return the choke control to normal as soon as the engine will run without 'lumpiness'. Find the speed at which your car seems happiest and decide upon this as your cruising speed. Economy driving does not imply that you are obliged to creep along at 20 mph most of the time. It is possible to drive quite briskly without wasting fuel. The secret is to stay in top gear as much as is possible without 'slogging' the engine, and to drive as if the brakes had failed; by this I mean that you will use what momentum you have to help you up the next hill or around the next bend without dissipating energy in a completely useless manner by excessive braking. You should be able to foresee when the engine is likely to labour on a hill and so change down in good time, at the same time avoiding enthusiastic acceleration. It is best to keep to the middle of the engine's speed range as much as possible. This is roughly between 2,500 and 3,500 rpm for most modern cars. If you wish to take really positive steps to improve your sense of economy driving, then it could pay to fit a vacuum gauge. Using this, you merely drive in such a manner as to maintain the maximum vacuum as far as you can. Such a gadget can save you quite a lot on your fuel bill.

Speaking of gadgets brings to mind the number of such things that are on the market today ranging in price from around £2 to well over £20. Sales talk claims that they help in various ways, such as limiting pressure surges in the fuel line, improving the spark quality or increasing carburettor efficiency and so on. The magazines *Motor*, *Autocar* and *Drive* have all tested them from time to time, but without significant results. They are best avoided, for good servicing and sensible driving are hard to beat, and wiser in the long run.

There are, however, other things which can be done to your engine to improve economy generally and fuel consumption in particular. One of the best is the thermostatically controlled electric fan, which replaces the belt-driven one fitted as standard in most cars. The belt-driven type rotates all the time and so absorbs an appreciable amount of power; it has been calculated that some 7-8 per cent of the engine's output at maximum revs is wasted. In Britain we need full fan functioning only when the car is stationary in traffic in warm weather, and it therefore makes sense to arrange matters so that the fan is controlled, making the most efficient use of it. There are several firms who market electric fan kits which can be fitted by the keen owner-driver, but it would be wise to take professional advice from your garage, since not all of them provide adequate cooling for all models of car.

All engines run best when properly warmed up without being too hot; the oil flows more freely and the fuel mixture vapourises more satisfactorily, improving petrol consumption. The running temperature of your engine is controlled by a thermostat which governs the flow of coolant to the engine. Ask your garage about fitting a thermostat designed to operate at a higher temperature than the one already fitted. It will be unlikely to cause overheating unless you tow a caravan or boat, or are planning a trip in a mountainous region during summer.

Transistorised ignition systems can help to reduce faults in the distributor circuit, and also maintain the tune of the engine for much longer periods than the conventional make-and-break points of the time-honoured system. The 'breakerless' types are probably the best in the long run, although the transistor assisted contact types, which use the existing contact breaker, greatly extend their useful life by effectively reducing the current which passes through them. The more advanced types of 'breakerless' ignition have either an electromagnetic, or optical, trigger which eliminate the contact breaker entirely.

If you wish to measure your fuel consumption accurately, don't rely on your fuel gauge; it is not intended to be an accurate instrument. Stand the car on a level forecourt at a garage you know, then fill the tank to neck of the filler cap, bouncing the car gently to eliminate bubbles and small airlocks. Zero the trip mileometer or record the mileage as accurately as you can. Now drive for at least 250 miles, since the greater the distance travelled between calculations, the more accurate will be the final figure. 1,000 miles would be ideal, and make for more accurate calculations. At the termination of the selected test distance, no matter how many gallons you may have added meanwhile, refill the tank to the neck of the filler cap exactly as you did originally, recording the quantity needed to the nearest tenth of a gallon. This quantity, plus what you added during the test, but not the original tankful, represents the total amount of fuel actually used by the car. Divide it into the number of miles covered during the period of the test, and you have the required figure showing consumption in miles per gallon. This takes into account your overall method of driving and averages everything out, including any tyre changes and so on which you may have found necessary. It does not, however, take into account any error there may be in the mileometer, although, of course, it is possible to check this for yourself against the motorway's hundred-metre posts (remember that each of these has two figures on it; one stating the kilometre and the other each successive tenth of a kilometre. Some of our speedometers are already calibrated in kilometres, but if yours is not, then you'll have to do yet another calculation — 1 km = 0.6214 mile).

The size and type of car you need depends on your own requirements, but is usually a compromise. For a fair amount of high-speed motorway or autobahn cruising obviously overdrive or a fifth gear is desirable, and experience has decided that a manual gearbox is usually more economical than an automatic. Bearing all this in mind, the layman is faced with a bewildering array of makes and models. Whichever you eventually pick, you'll very probably decide, after about a year, that you may have made a mistake and wish to try something else. Whatever you do decide, however, let it be your own decision, uninfluenced by friends, no matter of how long standing.

If your choice is a new car, there are three points to bear in mind:

1 read the driver's handbook very carefully and do exactly as the maker recommends; particularly with regard to running in;

2 should the car not be undersealed when you take delivery, then have it done as soon as possible. Preferably before you use it;

3 remember the maker's guarantee covers only components and poor workmanship. It does not usually cover labour if parts have to be replaced.

Should your choice be a used car, then there are also points to bear in mind. There are booklets published monthly which provide a guide to used car prices, and you will find typical current prices quoted in the back pages of some of the monthly motoring magazines. These are the prices you would expect to pay if you bought from a dealer. The monthly price guides categorise the cars into three main grades; these are:

First Class. Here the vehicle really should be in first-class condition, everything working efficiently and not needing any attention. Standard equipment and tools should be available and maintenance should have been regularly carried out. Mileage should not exceed roughly 12,000 per annum. Ask to see the servicing records, which should be available;

Average. Free from major damage; no serious distortion, looseness or corrosion on bodywork or chassis; brakes and lights in good condition; no oil or water leakage; steering, suspension and tyres good, but maybe a somewhat higher mileage than Class I vehicles, and perhaps not in quite such a good state of maintenance;

Below Average. These cars will show much more than the average mileage and will certainly not be up to the body or mechanical standards of the previous two classes, but should be in a good roadworthy condition.

Of course all categories should have a test certificate to authenticate their condition. Remember, though, that by law this is only really worth anything on the day you buy the vehicle. You could, for instance, be stopped by a police patrol car a week or so after you had bought it, and if they tested your brakes and found them inefficient, the ball would be in your court — not in that of the 'gentleman' from whom you bought the car.

In the end it really all comes down to what you can afford. Occasionally you will find a shark who tries to sell a car when perhaps some 30,000 or 40,000 miles are coming up — for the second time around — on the speedometer. He may assure you with a straight face and a steady eye that she's a genuine low-mileage bargain. Be suspicious. Do some detective work. Look at the carpets, the pedal rubbers; there may be no blemish on the paintwork, but such tricksters, unless they are in the trade, seldom think of such obvious things as pedal rubbers. If water has been oozing in, no matter how little, it will leave some traces under the carpets which are seldom moved. A good tip is to look under the bonnet. A chap who keeps the engine room reasonably clean and neat is likely to have looked after the other bits and pieces as well. Evidences of rust or corrosion under the wheel arches or sills are a warning sign that you should leave that one alone.

Should you be unfortunate enough to make a bad buy instead of the reliable vehicle you had hoped, remember that today you have the Trades Description Act on your side, and

54

you should, as soon as possible, inform your local inspector of weights and measures, upon whose shoulders falls the authority of upholding your rights for you. He will be grateful for full information and all the details you can provide at the outset. In view of the provisions of the Act, it would be wise to have a third party present before the deal is finalised, when you can ask the dealer, in the presence of your witness, if the mileage is correct, and whether he can personally vouch for the reliability of the car. Ask him, too, whether the car has ever been involved in an accident. He will be reluctant to make any false statement in the presence of a witness, since under the TDA it is a criminal offence to use a false or misleading statement, either written or spoken, in an attempt to make a sale.

Both the AA and the RAC operate systems whereby one of their inspectors will carry out an independent examination. You will receive a full written report from them, and it *is* a full report. Naturally he cannot be expected to check physically certain items such as the actual internal state of the engine or gearbox, but by running the car he can let you know whether they are, at that moment, in a reasonable condition for the age of the car.

When the TDA was first brought into force, traders declared they were being unmercifully persecuted, and that they daren't open their mouths for fear of incriminating themselves. Now, however, they join with the general public in praising it — at least the reputable ones do so.

According to statistics, the 'average' motorist drives some 12,000 miles a year, so provided you know the 'year letter' system, a gl e at the numberplates and a quick look at the speedometer will tell you whether a car is likely to be sold as a high- or low-mileage vehicle, and you can then expect the price to be in accordance with this fact.

Another point to bear in mind when changing cars is that if you do not regularly do a high mileage, then a larger vehicle will probably be more economical for you. The smaller cars such as Minis, Imps, and so on are less thirsty than the larger ones, and so are in greater demand, fetching higher prices when used. However, the depreciation on a larger car is usually less than that on a smaller one, and this will go quite a way towards offsetting the additional fuel expense. Besides, the market today could enable you to purchase a luxury car at used car rates which you might not otherwise have been able to afford. Third-party, fire and theft cover on such a car could cost less than comprehensive insurance on the smaller vehicle. All this is quite a consideration when one considers that the larger family saloons usually have a much more de-luxe specification than their smaller brethren.

Some models, following the example of taxis, offer the choice between petrol or diesel engines. On no account decide which you should have by merely comparing the cost of fuel, but consider carefully the use to which you intend to put the vehicle. Should it be your intention to cover some 20,000 miles a year or more, then a diesel-powered vehicle could save you money over a few years. Diesels tend to be somewhat noisier than petrol-operated vehicles and, when idling, vibration is usually much more noticeable; pollution from exhaust when the engine is pulling hard, as on steep hills, is also greater. There is also the consideration that they are harder to start on a really cold day, since the viscosity of the fuel oil increases with a drop in temperature. Then again, should you be unfortunate enough ever to drain the fuel tank completely, you may have to face a rather unexpected garage bill for cleaning the injectors and bleeding the system. This doesn't happen with a petrol engine.

Another type of engine that has gone in and out of fashion is the Wankel. In the conventional petrol engine each step takes place separately, ie each cylinder fires in turn, whereas, in the Wankel, one complete revolution of the rotor produces three power strokes. This seems, on the face of it, to be a tremendous bonus, but, like most things, one doesn't get something for nothing. The main difficulty is that of production, and in early prototypes the tips of the rotors were hard to design so that there could be an efficient seal maintained in order to effectively isolate the three chambers from each other whilst the rotor completed its complicated gyrations. Many materials were tried and at last the boffins settled on aluminium-impregnated carbon.

The first Wankel Spyder NSU appeared at the Frankfurt Motor Show in September 1963, and since then Toyo Kogo, makers of Mazda cars, have purchased manufacturing rights. There are now several models available with this type of power plant, and other manufacturers have got into the act. American manufacturers are also trying out the system, and there is at least one aircraft (the Curtiss-Wright) which has flown with it.

In the western world's present fuel position, the big attraction offered by the Wankel is the fact that it is capable of using the lowest grade fuel on the market. Unfortunately pollution level is by no means negligible, but the designers are still working on this.

One other minor point. For the early motorists, buying fuel was not the easy matter it is for us today, since only isolated shops stocked 'petroleum spirit' as it was known. Some drivers asked for 'petroleum oil', which was not petrol, but paraffin. If they had enough petrol in the tank already, the motor would run. Remembering this, drivers during World War II managed to run their cars on a paraffin cocktail. Modern cars, with their high compression ratios would dislike this — it is false economy, causes additional pollution, and is therefore quite illegal.

WINDS

Further minor considerations which affect the economy of motoring quite considerably are commonly overlooked by the majority of drivers; anything altering the streamlining, which has been the cause of considerable headaches on the part of its designer, may be legitimately regarded as an undesirable excrescence, and, if possible, should be eliminated. Examples are roof racks (which should only be fitted when they are actually to be used) and wing mirrors, for safety reasons a very desirable feature. In the case of wing mirrors, it pays to replace them, where possible, with the type designed for sports cars — to help reduce wind drag. A roof rack can reduce a car's overall speed by at least a couple of miles per hour, and anything which can do that is obviously increasing petrol consumption.

In addition to the economy factor, winds can frequently constitute something of a hazard in themselves, particularly at speed on exposed roads such as motorways. This applies more particularly to taller vehicles and those towing caravans or boats. The latter may often be seen yawing considerably when there are strong crosswinds. Of course it is not usually the winds in themselves which are the actual danger, for one subconsciously corrects their affect upon the vehicle by steering; it is gustiness which makes them really lethal. Proof of this may quite easily be observed, for instance, when a car passes under a bridge in the presence of a crosswind, or when overtaking a large lorry in the same conditions; one then has to actively correct the car's course by a pronounced additional pressure on the steering wheel.

The combined length when towing also increases the resistance to side winds and the 'time exposed to danger', as well — defined as the time spent out of one's own lane when overtaking or positioning for a right turn — and this should be borne in mind constantly.

CHAPTER FIVE

Driving in Adverse Conditions

YOUR MENTAL APPROACH

Mental preoccupation or lack of concentration caused by worry, distraction, or domestic troubles can render any driver accident-prone, no matter how good he may otherwise be. People who have been annoyed or upset in any way should therefore allow themselves a cooling-off period before taking a car on the road. The most fatal thing in this category is to actually lose one's temper while driving. A good driver is always aware of his own mental condition and makes due allowances for it, taking additional care when necessary. Remember that the manner in which a driver uses the power under his control shows his true character and just how mature he is.

Ice and Snow. Cold weather produces hazards which are infrequent at more pleasant times of the year, and the most common of these is a general misting-up of the windscreen and windows inside the car. A rear-window heater is not just a luxury; it is a desirable necessity if you are not to stop repeatedly in order to clear the rear window. Ventilation in cars has improved tremendously over the past couple of decades, but if the system in your car is not perfectly satisfactory it will help to open one or more windows slightly at the top. Half a potato rubbed over the inside of the windscreen will help to prevent it becoming misted, should your demister be inefficient or take a long time to warm up. This may seem to be an old wives' tale, but it works.

When ice or snow cover the ground they are an ever-present hazard, for the friction between tyres and road surface is then at its very lowest. Optimum grip for the prevailing conditions may be obtained by:

1 keeping your speed well below that which is suitable for dry roads;

2 using only gentle acceleration, braking and steering;

3 keeping your engine revs steady.

Above all, if you are not accustomed to driving in arctic conditions, treat the surface as you would if you were walking upon it. Be *very* cautious the first time you attempt this kind of driving; it is just too easy to slide and spin.

Above all, remember that stopping on an icy road is impossible to achieve within the same distance as on dry roads, so allow for this. One further point is that skid conditions do not occur only in winter. At almost any time of the year, if it has been dry for perhaps many days, a sudden shower of rain can induce very treacherous conditions even on good roads. During dry weather odd oily drips and splashes occur, and these are mixed with a film of shredded rubber from the thousands of tyres passing daily. The moment the rain commences this mixture of goo becomes perhaps worse than ice or snow — worse because you may be unprepared for it. Wet autumn leaves, loose gravel and partially repaired roads are other hazards of a similar type which you should be alert to notice. Snow and ice are visible as a rule (with the possible exception of the dreaded 'black ice') so the other conditions can be, and usually are, more dangerous, for they are more subtle and therefore much more treacherous.

Fog and Poor Visibility. When these are the prevailing conditions, take your car out only if your journey is absolutely essential, unless of course you enjoy playing blind man's buff with a ton or more of lethal machinery.

When forced to venture forth, switch on dipped headlights (sidelights under these conditions are futile). If you have a foglamp train it on the nearside kerb. Should a spotlight or second foglamp be fitted, adjust it so that it shines only just ahead of your front wheels, sufficient for you to see the cats' eyes. Be fairly accurate with this or you will dazzle oncoming traffic.

Travel at such a speed that you are able to stop safely well within the distance you can see to be clear.

Before bringing the car to a halt, dab the brake pedal several times sufficient to actuate the 'stop' lights without causing the car to jerk, and this will alert the following traffic to your intentions. Arm signals might not be seen, and a flashing red light is a prominent display, even in fog. While we are on this subject, don't be tempted to follow the rear lights of other traffic too blindly, or you could, perhaps, find yourself following another chap into his garage.

Above all *never* assume that the road ahead is clear — this is how those catastrophic multiple collisions on motorways occur. Allow plenty of room between yourself and the car in front, so that you can stop safely if he has to do so unexpectedly.

The increasing tendency of some local authorities to skimp on cats' eyes is to be greatly deprecated; the white paint they use as a substitute does not save so many lives by a long way. When you are groping your way homewards through atrocious visibility, open your windows and switch off the radio, because that helps you to hear the presence of other traffic.

Should you be the first car in a queue, you will cleave some sort of slight clearance through the fog, lulling following drivers into a false sense of security. One may become impatient as a result, and try to overtake. Let him do so as safely as you can by holding well in to the near side. When he takes his turn at pathfinding the last laugh will be yours. There is one possible pitfall here; he may not realise that the visibility is quite as bad as you did, and may try to pull back in again. So long as you are aware of this possibility, all should be well.

Have the windscreen wipers working and the washers in good operative condition always, so that mud splashes may be cleared immediately.

Carbon Monoxide. This is a far greater factor in causing accidents than is popularly supposed. Faulty exhaust systems; imperfect flooring; the older type of heater systems, if not in top condition; seals between body and engine compartments, and so on can all represent potential CO dangers to the unwary driver, and are points to check carefully.

It is wise to close front ventilators when standing in traffic queues with other vehicles whose engines are idling.

Perhaps you have drilled holes in the front bulkhead in order to facilitate the fitting of auxiliary dials or other accessories. If so, make sure that a properly fitting grummet is inserted, both to act as additional electrical insulation and to ensure the exclusion of CO, besides, of course, just keeping out draughts.

Fords and Floods. Fords are still encountered occasionally, while floods can happen at any time. Drivers who are fond of lanes and byways are naturally more likely to meet with this kind of hazard, but it pays to be prepared.

The accepted method is to reduce speed considerably, change to a lower gear and proceed slowly through what appears to be the shallowest part of the water — usually the crown of the road. Try to use such a speed that no splashes enter the engine compartment and keep the engine ticking over just fast enough to prevent ingress of water at the exhaust causing back pressure. Once clear of the water, and having negotiated the far bank or slope, test the brakes as soon as possible. Should they not be as effective as usual either drive for a short time with one foot lightly on the brake pedal, or dab it repeatedly until you can feel considerable improvement. The heat generated by this treatment will very soon dry them out.

Should the engine fail before clearing the flooded section, the car may often be driven out on the starter motor, using the lowest gear. It will make this operation easier, if you don't mind getting your feet wet, to remove the sparking plugs first; it will also be a lot kinder to your battery. When on dry ground, the electrical system may be dried out, paying particular attention to the plugs and their leads, the ignition coil and the distributor cap. Remove this last item, and dry it thoroughly inside and out before even attempting to restart, or your battery may become exhausted.

NIGHT DRIVING

Even though one's daytime vision may be normal, difficulty may possibly be experienced in seeing objects clearly at night. Glaring headlights also complicate the matter and, after oncoming cars have passed, even on dipped lights, some time is required for vision to return to absolute normal. Anything at all which reduces the small amount of light entering the eye at night should be avoided, and for this reason all windscreens, windows and rear light glasses should be meticulously clean. There has been proof that anti-glare devices are a potential danger, especially to those with the slightest vision defect.

A further point is that the age of drivers is important so far as night vision is concerned, since the ability to see in dim light diminishes with age. Older eyes are slower to recover from glare, since the older one is, the slower the retina adjusts to varying light levels. For these reasons, the following is good advice:

1 drive at an overall lower speed than in the daytime;

2 drive at night only when thoroughly rested — fatigue impairs vision;

3 know the range of your headlights, and drive at such a speed that you can stop well within this distance;

4 do not use dark or tinted glasses — these impair night vision;

5 reduce speed in the face of oncoming traffic, and avoid looking directly at lights, even when dipped;

6 in the face of oncoming lights, concentrate on the pool of darkness between them and the nearside kerb — it is there where cyclists, pedestrians and so on may be expected;

7 dip lights when following other cars;

8 maintain battery, lights and all electrical apparatus in good condition;

9 do not allow the use of lights inside your own car;

10 check the adjustment of your headlights periodically;

11 keep headlights and all other glasses on the car spotlessly clean.

It is axiomatic that physical fitness in a driver ensures alertness. The slightest change in one's physical state, colds, headaches, toothache, or mental wellbeing in general can result in a reduction of vigilance, clarity of vision and power of judgement. The cumulative result is a perceptible reduction in reaction time, which could be the cause of an accident. It is remarkable that a totally deaf person who is aware of his disability soon develops his other senses to make up for his defect, and uses them to be even more alert and cautious as a consequence. Nevertheless anyone who is not in the best of his customary health should not attempt to drive. If circumstances force him to do so, then greatly reduced speed, an increased hangback distance and exceptional caution should enable him to make up for his low condition.

ALCOHOL

Since October 1967, motorists in Great Britain have been subject to a legal maximum limit of the amount of alcohol permissible in their blood. Prior to that date any laws aspiring to precision existed only on the continent and in the United States. Despite considerable publicity, however, the average person still has little idea of the facts behind the law. Alcoholic liquors have always had their opponents as well as their protagonists, but fortunately most countries are now passing through an enlightened period where alcohol is more or less socially acceptable. Extensive tests established the fact that 80mg of alcohol per 100ml of blood was a reasonable amount upon which to base legislation, and this is now enforced by means of the 'breathalyser' which is used by the police for screening purposes in cases where they have reason to believe that a driver is in charge of a vehicle whilst under the influence of drink. Prosecution is not usually brought on the evidence supplied by this alone. It is used merely as justification for the police to demand a blood or urine sample for further quantitative study, and further proceedings are taken only if the chemical tests upon these samples indicate an alcohol content above the legal level.

As the law stands, a sober driver, after a collision with an inebriated cyclist, may be given a breath test on the spot whilst the cyclist is perfectly safe from the verdict of any breathalyser, since the law makes no mention of cyclists whatever. Unfortunately, the motorist is increasingly singled out for restrictive treatment of a specialist nature, although pedestrians and cyclists are involved in a very large number of accidents. Road safety is the realm of the Department of Transport, but responsibility for the enforcement of laws concerning it is the realm of the Home Office and science is having an ever-increasing say in both.

A sensible law brought into force with effect from 23 March

1975 states that drivers are required to switch lights on in poor daytime visibility — whether caused by fog, smoke, heavy rain, mist, spray or snow. Nearly all four-wheeled vehicles will have to use sidelights plus headlamps, a pair of foglamps or a matched pair of fog and spotlamps. It is left to the discretion of the driver to decide just when to switch on, but in such circumstances it is better to be too early than too late. Sidelamps by themselves in poor visibility are worse than useless.

Another good law, introduced two days later, governed the use of direction indicators which can be used simultaneously as a hazard warning. It has been amended to state that such indicators may now be used only when the vehicle is stationary on a road and when the intention is to warn other road users of a temporary obstruction on the highway, or, if the vehicle is a public service vehicle, whether stationary or not, for the purpose of summoning assistance for the driver, conductor or an inspector.

It is now also quite legal to sound the horn on a public service vehicle at any time, even when stationary, in order to summon assistance for the crew.

One very useful exercise on the part of any government with the courage of its convictions would be to have the entire set of road traffic acts cleaned up and rewritten in the light of contemporary experience. The Road Safety Act 1967 is really an extension to the Road Traffic Act 1960, and with other related modifications these are known collectively as the Road Traffic Act 1960-7. The Road Traffic Act 1962 lays down disqualification for various offences, other road traffic acts prior and subsequent to these affect us in a host of other ways, and the average motorist has little or no access to these in the normal course of events. In theory he may break a law which he does not even know exists. When the present Act (in all its ramifications) is rewritten it would certainly be a great idea if this and all the other earlier acts and amendments could be consolidated into a single concise and intelligible act in order that motorists as a whole could be clearer concerning their responsibilities to themselves, the public and their passengers. As things are now the numerous road traffic acts all contain separate and distinct special sections which alter or repeal earlier acts in part or in whole.

GENERAL

Roads and vehicles are steadily improving all the time, and to say that either a road or a vehicle was responsible for a collision is manifestly incorrect. What really happened was that the vehicle was being driven at the time of the collision in a manner which was unsafe for the prevailing conditions or for that particular vehicle, or perhaps that it was imperfectly maintained. There are certain drivers who use roads correctly at all times and others who use them badly. A minority of drivers seem to take risks for the sake of taking them, and your job as an advanced driver is to be able to recognise these and keep out of their accidents. These are the people who ditch their cars, follow too close to your rear bumper, overtake and immediately turn left/right, perform manoeuvres un-expectedly without use of mirror or signals, and pull out from the kerb without warning.

Major car manufacturers in all countries are going very carefully into the matter of safety for the occupants of cars in the event of a collision, but a car incorporating all the possible permutations of their findings would be far beyond the purses of most people. All cars now, however, have safety belts fitted, and these should be worn on every occasion the car is taken on the road. The manufacturers of car chemicals are also pretty active and, in addition to the well known de-icers, there are also sprays which deter damp on the electrical system, prime the carburettor for easy starting, remove tar and similar blemishes, reflate punctured tyres and repair the puncture. There is even a spray which claims to eliminate wheelspin on snow or ice to a certain extent. One of the most useful chemicals is an additive to the windscreen washing water, which shifts the goo caused by squashed insects, oil and traffic fumes like magic.

CHAPTER SIX

Forces to Contend With

From what has already been said, and from personal experience, it will be realised that as soon as a car moves there are certain forces acting upon it. When it begins to move, initial inertia has to be overcome; when it is being brought to a stop by braking, the centre of gravity shifts forward, causing the nose to dip; acceleration causes a shift in the opposite direction, and, of course, in corners and bends centrifugal force tries to take charge.

The good driver is aware of this, and drives with it in mind at all times, except perhaps when carrying out minor manoeuvres at slow speeds, such as parking.

There are, of course, more complex forces at work from time to time, when climbing or descending hills, or driving over very uneven ground. All this constitutes a very sound reason for taking things steadily when driving a strange vehicle for the first time. As one becomes more used to the 'feel' of it, one can begin to handle it with a somewhat greater degree of nonchalance.

The most obvious force experienced by even the inexperienced driver is perhaps centrifugal, and he usually encounters it when he has taken a bend or corner at a speed higher than he had estimated safe for that particular hazard. This is why police, public transport authorities and so on have skid pans and use them as part of driver training. On such a surface, breakaway occurs much earlier than on a normal dry road, with the result that less driving time has to be spent there in order to acquire practice and skill. It would be a good idea to enquire where your nearest skid pan is to be found, who is responsible for it, and whether it is available to the general public. Usually the road safety officer for your area will be able to help in this respect, and may even be able to book a session for you. It will help if you can get one or two friends interested, and perhaps share a block booking which is bound to be more economical. Sometimes a go-ahead driving school has access to such facilities. If so you are lucky, for the instructor responsible for the area will have stacked a few piles of old tyres here and there in a sort of planned chaos in order to provide artificial hazards. The best way to deal with skid pans, if it is your first time on one, is to let one driver go out first and try his paces, first driving around sedately, then increasing speed gradually as he begins to weave between the obstructions. When he comes in to get his breath, the next car can try. Follow this by two cars playing 'follow my leader', then, if you dare, let others join in — provided the pan is large enough and the drivers show adequate progress in car handling under these conditions.

Novice pupils who have received skid-control instruction on skid pans have been grateful for the experience when the next winter has provided arctic conditions for them to deal with in earnest. Many have been able to stay on the road and keep their vehicles going when those around them were either sliding off the road or into each other, and coping with wheelspin and other horrors. The skid control 'experts' knew just what to do, and got home safely. A good idea in such conditions is to carry a shovel and one or two old sacks in the boot of the car, by the way.

Centrifugal force acting on a car on a bend provides the best reason of all for braking well before the bend, and entering it at the speed you have decided will be safe. Imagine what happens when a driver brakes in the bend itself. The car already has a tendency to slide outwards. Braking throws the weight forward, so that most of the strain is thrown on the front tyre on the outside of the bend; the others are relieved of a great deal of weight, and therefore have less grip on the road, so a skid becomes a distinct probability—whilst all this is happening, the poor outside front tyre may be nearing bursting point, dependent upon how seriously it is being maltreated.

On the other hand, correct braking before the bend, to such a speed that it may be entered under slight acceleration, results in the car's weight being transferred rearwards under the acceleration—more weight on the rear wheels give them a better grip, reducing skid risk, and the front tyres are relieved of the possibility of disaster, besides making steering itself easier. The moral is, therefore, enter slowly and leave fast, increasing one's speed as opposed to decreasing it whilst in the bend.

It will be realised, of course, that front-wheel and rear-wheel drive cars behave differently in corners. The best way to find out the actual difference in handling between the two types is to try them out for yourself. It will be found that the front-wheel drive tends to 'oversteer', or take a bend rather tightly, whilst the opposite is true for the rear-wheel drive car. This may sound alarming to the tyro, but actual practice reveals that there is nothing to worry about unduly, for one soon becomes accustomed to the change from one to the other and compensates instinctively. The front-wheel drive does have one main advantage in awkward situations, and that is that the weight of the engine, battery and other heavy components is right over the driving wheels of the car, which assists road grip. This means that in mud or snow it will be

71

much easier to pull free, and there will be less liability for wheelspin to occur. One doesn't need to have a sack of coal in the boot at the onset of winter in order to eliminate wheelspin.

There is yet another set of circumstances which is a prolific source of accidents. The rear-end collision is, according to the insurance companies, one of the most common causes of loss of no claims discount. The main reason for this is driving too close to the car in front in poor road conditions, so that when the rear car brakes, his wheels lock and he slides into the car ahead. The reason they locked was that he was far too close in the first place and as a result had to brake far harder than should have been necessary. In such a case there is no room to take avoiding action by steering, and in any case such action would, on a slippery surface, probably result in an even more complex skid, and maybe even multi-vehicular damage. Since prevention is much better than cure, the answer is to heed the section of the *Highway Code* which advises drivers always to adopt such speed that they can stop well within the distance they can see to be clear. In such conditions that will result in intact NCDs for both drivers.

Even should the worst happen, and you find yourself sliding into the car in front, remember that the cause is too harsh an application of the brakes, and that the cure for any skid is to remove its cause. Release the brake pedal immediately and 'pump' it, using what is called 'cadence' braking. This results in a series of maximum braking effect applications on all wheels, since maximum braking obviously occurs just before the wheels lock. This may not, perhaps, completely prevent a collision, but it will certainly result in a much less serious one — maybe the difference between broken headlamp glasses and extensive mechanical or physical damage. It will still not save your NCD, however, if you are the rear driver concerned, for he is always held to be the one to blame, and rightly so, for a driver's first duty is to avoid the danger ahead of him.

Cars are designed to travel normally in a straight line, which is why their steering geometry is so arranged that if you release the wheel in a corner, the front wheels will automatically try to resume their 'straight ahead' position. You have to misalign them deliberately in order to steer the car in a curve. Many drivers take advantage of this to let the steering wheel slip through their hands on the 'recovery'. This in itself is a bad habit, for jerkiness, however slight, is to be avoided for mechanical reasons as well as those of car control. Should you take any of the tests mentioned in Chapter Seven, the examiner will certainly fault you on this count. Crossing the hands on the steering wheel, ie permitting the left hand to go to the right of 12 o'clock and 6 o'clock on the wheel, is also frowned upon by some examiners, and may even result in failure of the test, particularly if there are any other faults noted. What examiners look for is a method of steering which may be described as fluent or fluid, depending upon his views upon such things. Their own standards are absolutely rigid, and consistent throughout the country, so that all candidates will have an equal and fair test. One thing that all examiners have in common is that they like to see smooth and competent driving, and one of the points which affect this most is gear-changing.

Gone are the days when double-declutching was a necessity which one was obliged to master in order to deal properly with the 'crash' gearboxes before the blessings of 'synchromesh'. There are still many cars, however, on which no synchromesh is provided on first gear. If you are driving such a car the examiner may justly ask you to reduce speed (not below about 5-10 mph) and change to first gear. To do this noiselessly and efficiently, one should use the double-declutching technique. Here it is, briefly:

1 release the accelerator and simultaneously depress the clutch pedal;

2 select neutral and release the clutch pedal, accelerate;

3 depress the clutch pedal and select first gear;

73

4 release the clutch pedal as you accelerate.

The whole thing should be done quickly and smoothly, and with practice can be carried out as quickly as a straightforward gear change.

'Heel and toe changes' are occasionally referred to in this context. This really means that when it is necessary to brake and change to a lower gear at the same time, maybe when approaching a ticklish bend, or descending a steep hill, you may carry out the following procedure: use the right foot to accelerate whilst holding the footbrake on at the same time; the left foot does its customary ballet on the clutch pedal as usual. In a few cars the pedals are so placed as to make this procedure difficult, so make sure that you can do it easily and safely before attempting it in a nasty spot.

A refined sense of acceleration is a useful asset, for a driver who understands the relationship between speed and distance can obviously commence to accelerate for overtaking whilst an oncoming car is still passing the vehicle ahead of his own. In this manoeuvre, of course, it is always wise to commence the overtaking procedure whilst well astern of the car you intend to overtake, for not only does it give a better view ahead, but by the time you are actually overtaking, you have built up a safe and satisfactory speed to pass quickly and return to your own lane as soon as it becomes safe to do so. Consequently the 'time exposed to danger' (the time you are out of your own lane, in the centre of the road) will be considerably reduced.

On most cars the trackrods are so adjusted that the wheels toe in by a small amount, but with some they should be set parallel, and with others the designer has deliberately toed them out. The workshop manual for your model will tell you just what is what, and by how much your wheels should be offset, if at all. Faulty wheel alignment is very soon revealed by uneven wear on the tyre treads. Often it is caused by careless parking and striking the kerb with the nearside front wheel. In addition to tyre wear this can cause wheel wobble, indicated by a violent shaking of the steering wheel at certain speeds. Excessive wear or looseness in the steering system can also be a cause of wobble, as can badly balanced wheels. Wheel balancing is carried out by the attachment of small lead weights to the complete wheel and tyre assembly in order that the weight of the whole is evenly distributed. Badly balanced front wheels cause steering wheel vibration, and if it is the rear ones which are at fault then vibration is usually felt through the seats. Balancing should be carried out ideally whenever a tyre is replaced, and should be entrusted to a garage possessing proper dynamic balancing equipment.

Should you ever have the misfortune to drive a car which actually wanders or weaves from side to side, the steering system is badly in need of attention; the fault is usually due to excessive wear in the linkage or swivel pins, undue play on the wheel bearings, or uneven tyre pressures.

CHAPTER SEVEN

The Advanced Driving Organisations

There are several of these, all without doubt excellent bodies with splendid aims and objects. Two of them, the Institute of Advanced Motorists and the League of Safe Drivers, recruit their examiners from ex-police drivers or instructors, and the National Advanced Drivers Association may be said to train their own, since theirs are appointed from the cream of their superior driving assessment (the equivalent of the old gold star qualification). In addition there is the High Performance Club which is run by the BSM, and who appoint their own instructors and examiners.

No matter which organisation one decides to join, an advanced test must first be passed. My advice is to go for the most difficult. Not only is this the greatest challenge, but affords the most fun, and provides a sense of achievement.

Candidates for any of the tests, good drivers though they may be already, should pay particular attention to a few points which will impress the examiner favourably. Be punctual; if necessary reconnoitre the route to the test rendezvous beforehand. Dress smartly; have the car immaculate, with all windows sparkling; seat-belts worn by you and laid ready for the examiner; not the slightest doubt about the legality of tyre treads; all lights, indicators, wipers and so on checked for efficiency; no litter lying around inside the car; don't smoke while driving, and don't lounge around with one arm leaning on the window ledge.

Figure 6   Car badge of The League of Safe Drivers. A button affixed in the centre of the star indicates by its colour the grade of pass achieved by the member

LEAGUE OF SAFE DRIVERS

In February 1955 the League of Safe Drivers was founded by a Road Safety Committee in north London with the help of police driving instructors from the Metropolitan Police Driving School at Hendon, and by 1959 it was obvious that the league was giving a service that was of interest to a far wider public than the original membership.

The Northumberland Safe Drivers' Association had been active for some time, and had given considerable encouragement and assistance to the new league — they designed the league's badge and motto: *non nobis solum* (not for ourselves alone). The Northumberland Safe Drivers'

Association was eventually absorbed into the league in 1961.

Just prior to this, in 1960, the league became a nationwide organisation and a company, limited by guarantee, was formed to manage its finances. Test centres were established in many parts of Great Britain and membership has grown very steadily over the years. Since the formation of the company it has been registered as a charity.

All examiners hold a Police Class 1 Certificate or a Police Instructor's Certificate, and diploma courses are held in most large cities once or twice each year in order to give driving instructors advice concerning advanced driving tuition.

To take an advanced driving test applicants are required to drive for about one hour under normal traffic conditions accompanied by an examiner; the route is selected to include various types of road conditions and traffic situations varying from town to country. The examiner will expect you to drive quite normally, as you are being tested upon your everyday driving capabilities. During the test, which is not designed to catch you out, you will find him extremely helpful. His main object, besides testing your driving ability, is to put you completely at ease. Inherently safe drivers are eligible for membership.

In addition to the practical part of the test the examiner will ask questions designed to reveal your knowledge and understanding of the current *Highway Code* and your appreciation of your vehicle's steering, braking, tyres, lighting and so on, although no really technical knowledge is expected.

A few days after the test you will receive a copy of the test form including the examiner's comments; this is so that you will be able to study it and improve your standard of driving.

As a member of the league you will be entitled to display the distinctive car badge which bears a central button indicating the class of pass which you achieved — gold for class 1; silver for class 2; bronze for class 3. You will also receive a membership card and a certificate.

At regular intervals members receive the league's newsletter, and may also join in group visits to such places of interest as pre-driver training centres, the road research laboratory, police driving schools and skidpans as well as being able to attend such meetings and film shows as are periodically organised in the various areas. The league has an arrangement with the Eagle Star Insurance Group whereby members are entitled to generous discounts on their motor and other insurances. There is also a social side. For a nominal fee — usually around 50p, you will be able to join one of the social clubs or groups which operate in and around most large centres; their activities include the organisation of rallies, safe driving trials, films, lectures, dances and dinners. Enquiries should be addressed to:

Organising Secretary,
The League of Safe Drivers,
17 Holmwood Gardens,
LONDON
N3 3NS.

THE INSTITUTE OF ADVANCED MOTORISTS

In March 1956, as a result of suggestions from the late Lord Sempill, pioneer aviator and dedicated motorist, and a small number of other interested people, the Institute of Advanced Motorists was formed and registered as a non-profit-earning company, limited by guarantee, having as its objects:

1 to improve the standards of driving and the advancement of road safety;

2 to establish an advanced driving test.

The public soon came forward voluntarily for the assessment of their driving skills and to find out if their performance behind the wheel reached the standard required by the new body.

The advanced test was based upon the experience gained by

79

Figure 7   Car badge of the Institute of Advanced Motorists

the Metropolitan Police drivers, trained at Hendon in advanced driving since 1935. By practising their higher skills and efficiency their accident rate had dropped by 89 per cent in 1954, and it was this more than anything else which had caused Mr John Boyd Carpenter, in a public speech during November 1954, to state that 'a higher standard of skill and proficiency on the part of drivers could help to reduce accidents'.

Now nearly 200,000 tests have been carried out, mainly in private cars, although rigid commercial vehicles may be used, and motorcycle tests have begun. The standard of the test is based upon the police system as taught in Home Office Approved Police Driving Schools. The examiners, who are retired from the police force, have to hold a Class I police driving certificate, and the test routes, of which there are now seventy-two, are designed to provide all types of driving (except motorway) conditions. They are about 35 miles long, and the test takes roughly 1½ hours, with a half-hour 'debriefing' period at the end.

Approximately 80 per cent of the first-time failures return

for a re-test, and of these about 85 per cent pass at the second attempt, after correcting the faults which the examiner pointed out on their first test.

The IAM say that the pass rate for men and women is 62 per cent. Since its inauguration, some 116,500 members have been admitted, and there are, at the moment of writing, about 70,000 paid-up members.

Arising out of the main membership, some sixty members' groups have formed in the vicinity of the test routes, and about 10 per cent of members belong to a group. These groups were encouraged to form by the Ministry of Transport (as it used to be called) because of the great help they gave to local road safety officers, but, in addition, local groups do a great deal to further interest in good driving and in recruiting the public as members of the advanced organisations. At least three of the groups perform a very much appreciated service in training substantial numbers of disabled drivers at the request of the Department of Health and Social Security.

The IAM staff lecture to the public and in schools on road safety subjects, and has co-operated in the production of three highly successful road safety films.

The council is controlled by a body of people elected because of their expertise in various spheres of motoring, and who represent accident prevention authorities, medicine, motor racing, the motor industry, driving schools, magistrates, the motoring press and other motoring organisations. The list includes several members of Parliament, and the institute's activities have been endorsed by several transport ministers since its foundation.

Anyone with a full British driving licence may take the test, provided he or she has not been convicted of a traffic offence within the past three years, and with almost any car, truck, three-wheeler and, lately, motorcycles. Disabled drivers may also be tested provided they use a suitably modified vehicle. Tests are available from Monday to Friday each week and candidates are requested to meet the examiner at a prearranged rendezvous of mutual convenience near one of the test routes.

Displays of fancy driving are not expected; the examiners hope you will handle the car with a steady, workmanlike technique in the way you should normally drive every day. They do not like exaggeratedly low speeds or excessive signalling; they do like to see candidates observe all speed limits and drive with due regard to road, traffic and weather conditions, but they also want to see them drive briskly and not be afraid to cruise at the legal limit when circumstances permit. You will, of course, be asked to reverse round a corner and make a hill start, and there will certainly be one or two checks upon your powers of observation. There are, however, no trick questions, no attempts to catch you out, and you are not even required to give a running commentary at any time (although of course you are free to do so if you choose). Personally I would recommend all candidates to do a voluntary commentary. No examiner is a mind reader; he can only assess your performance upon what he observes for himself. You will, therefore, make his task much easier if you do a commentary. After all, the fact that you saw no reason to slow below 30 mph for those last few shops (or something!) doesn't necessarily imply you are a rash driver — you knew it was early closing day, but did he? Maybe he lives fifty or more miles away and doesn't have as much local knowledge as you. Make sure he knows just *why* you do things, and doesn't have to guess, for he might guess wrong. He wants to be quite fair to you and all other candidates, so give him the chance.

The following are the seven most prevalent reasons for failure in the test, according to the IAM. Each fault *by itself* might be insufficient to cause failure in the test, and these are only the result of analyses of unsuccessful tests. (The figures given are percentages.)

78 *Hazard procedures and cornering* — incorrect assessment, poor safety margin, unsystematic procedure.

72 *Use of gears* — late selection, intermediate gears not used to advantage.

70 *Positioning* — straddling lanes; incorrect for R and L turns.

60 *Braking* — late application, harshness; use of brakes and gears together.

58 *Distance observation* — late planning and assessment of traffic situation.

48 *Method of approach* — too fast; coasting; wrong lanes.

48 *Clutch control* — riding clutch; slipping it; coasting.

CAR AND MOTORCYCLE DRIVERS ASSOCIATION

An extremely dedicated driver, the late Ted Lambert, author of *Safe Driving for All, Steering Clear, Plan for Safer Roads* and many other works which have now become classics of motoring literature, saw the need for an advanced driving organisation which, unlike others, provided a graded series of tests. In 1958, therefore, together with several others of the same mind, he founded the Car and Motorcycle Drivers Association and formulated a carefully thought-out plan which was different to any that had gone before. The tests ranged from an extremely simple written paper, through what was called the silver star test (which resembled the standard advanced tests of the other two organisations), another written test, much more searching in nature, and which took no less than three hours to complete, and ended with a 300 mile night drive followed by manoeuvring tests off the road against the clock. A candidate who obtained over the specified number of marks in tests 3 and 4 qualified for the gold star award, which entitled him to wear a small golden star over his distinctive car badge.

The new organisation caught on and, over the next fifteen years, went from strength to strength with a steadily growing membership. The CAMDA examiners were appointed from the ranks of those who had achieved the accolade of the gold star. Unfortunately, like a number of lesser motor clubs, members found it difficult during the acute fuel shortage to maintain their obligations and, as a direct result of the country's financial situation, this organisation regrettably passed away on 31 December 1975.

Figure 8   Car badge of the National Advanced Drivers Association

NADA

There were, however, quite a few loyal souls who decided that it was just not good enough for such a promising organisation to fade into obscurity and vanish completely. Before CAMDA had wound up finally, they put their heads together and founded a logical successor to the parent organisation. The new association was named the National Advanced Drivers Association on 1 January 1976. Now spreading rapidly nationwide, it combines all the best concepts of advanced driving while bringing forceful answers to all the arguments

84

against advanced driving tests. NADA offers a complete assessment from the time of passing the DoT driving test, through a 'silver' assessment in the middle range (similar to the old CAMDA silver star) on to the really complex and difficult theoretical and practical gold assessment, for the driver who really wishes to be at the top of the class. A concession to the high price of motoring today is that the gold award no longer necessitates the 300 mile night drive followed by manoeuvring tests against the clock. It is now a carefully planned run over a rather difficult course which includes all types of road and traffic conditions plus a few special manoeuvres which the examiner may require. In this respect the old gold award holders who qualified with CAMDA may possibly consider the new gold award an easier qualification to acquire, but then isn't this an extension of the same 'old soldier' attitude which applies to almost everything?

The new silver award may be taken every three years, free of extra charge, after passing the assessment the first time. This enables a driver to keep his driving at a high standard even if he never attempts the gold.

There is free membership of local groups, a very warm welcome to all lady drivers, and the sixteen year old is encouraged to join and learn good driving habits even before he is actually allowed by law to handle today's powerful cars and motorcycles.

Further details and application forms may be obtained from:

The General Secretary,
The National Advanced Drivers Association,
2 Queensway,
Sawston,
CAMBRIDGE
CB2 4DJ.

A point of interest to former CAMDA members is that they retain any qualifications they earned under the auspices of

CAMDA and also their advanced driving licence, issued by that organisation. This was a useful document, forming a complete record of a driver's motoring history, including not only all the advanced tests he may have passed, but also any outstanding feats in the field of motoring, ie rallies, races, hillclimbs, unusual drives and expeditions, publications in the motoring press and so on. The National Advanced Drivers Association may continue the tradition, but, until fresh advanced licences are issued to members, the old ones, where applicable, will be brought up to date when submitted to headquarters.

Membership of the new organisation is growing swiftly, and examiners cover most of the country, so that potential candidates for the tests will not in any particular instance have very far to travel in order to attend their test.

The revised tests are as follows:

Improver Driver Assessment (bronze award). Consists of a ½ hour drive in your car with a NADA examiner who will point out and instruct you in the basic ideals of advanced driving, while assessing your own potential in this most important field of driving. Can be taken at any time in your driving career, but is especially useful if taken within a year of passing the DoT test.

Advanced Driving Assessment (silver award). A 1½ hour drive in your car within 20 miles of your home, your driving being assessed by a NADA examiner. After the drive, you receive from head office a written assessment of your driving. Those who reach the required standard will receive the silver qualification and be eligible to carry the NADA grille badge.

Theoretical Assessment. Is a written paper designed to explore your knowledge of the *Highway Code*, breakdowns, adverse weather conditions, general, motorway and country driving and similar matters.

Superior Driving Assessment. Consists of a 2 hour drive in your car with a NADA examiner in an area at least 50 miles from your home. A very high standard of driving is required and assessment of all road hazards will be expected.

Gold Award. This grading will not be easily earned, and is to be regarded as the accolade of the private motorist. Normally no attempt should be made to qualify for it until after passing the silver assessment, or its equivalent unless you belong to one of the other advanced driving organisations. The award is made to those candidates with a pass in the silver assessment and a pass in the theoretical assessment.

In addition to other benefits, membership entitles one to a free quarterly *Motoring Digest*, a vote in the election of the governing body at general meetings, free entry to yearly motoring conventions, reduced rates for the various NADA assessment tests, a free NADA car sticker, and a free re-test at the silver assessment grade every three years.

Upon acquiring the silver award, one is eligible for election to the governing body.

Examiners are normally selected from those members who hold the gold award of either CAMDA or NADA, and who have, in addition, a distinguished driving career.

THE HIGH PERFORMANCE CLUB

The High Performance Club was established in 1961, membership being restricted to people who achieve a high standard of driving skill whilst undergoing the British School of Motoring high performance course. The BSM itself was formed in 1910.

The course is designed to help good drivers to become expert, and to provide even the most expert drivers with that final polish. In every case it is tailored to your own individual needs and is aimed at helping you to gain the utmost pleasure and satisfaction from your car and your own driving skill.

The course starts from the British School of Motoring offices at 102 Sydney Street, Chelsea SW3, and is divided into three sessions of 3½ hours, 6½ hours and 7 hours respectively.

During the three sessions, driving on every type of road is covered including motorways, trunk roads, country lanes, suburban roads and circuit work, together with some skid-control instruction. The skid-road facilities at the Jim Russell Racing School at Snetterton are used, and circuit work is carried out at the Cadwell Park Circuit. The last two stages of the course must be taken on consecutive days, as the trainees stay overnight at the George Hotel, Spilsby in Lincolnshire.

You will be accompanied by a highly skilled co-driver throughout the course. At his discretion you may use your own car if you wish. Should you do so, a discount of £1 per hour is allowed.

Figure 9   Car badge of the BSM High Performance Course graduate

Grand touring cars and fast saloon cars are rapidly becoming more and more popular. Their performance is also becoming more vivid, and a large number of people are painfully aware that their own driving falls far short of the performance of their cars. For this reason the British School of Motoring have introduced a special 10½ hour 'gran tourismo' course which aims to teach you to drive GT cars with the maximum enjoyment and the maximum level of safety. This course is also divided into three sessions which cover driving on all types of road.

Both the high performance and the gran tourismo courses

are classed as advanced driving courses, and nearly 1,500 people have now qualified as high performance club members, of which almost 150 are ladies. These courses attract approximately fifty-two aspirants per year, of which number some two-thirds take the high performance course.

Incidentally the BSM also runs other specialised courses, such as the chauffeurs' course, anti-hi-jack course, and specialised instruction on clients' own vehicles where requested. Although these hardly count as conventional advanced driving courses, they are, nevertheless, worth recording here on account of their specialised nature.

There are special arrangements for those members of the HPC who wish to take occasional extra drives in order to maintain their high standard of driving.

THE POLICE FORCES

These have advanced driving schools at major centres throughout the country for the purpose of training the drivers of their patrol cars, incident units, and officers who specialise in traffic duties. Although it would be a great benefit to the public if police schools could accept pupils for these courses, it would be impractical for them to do so, since they are staffed only with police training in mind.

Many enlightened heads of police traffic departments, however, do arrange series of lectures from time to time, which the driver who is keen to improve his theoretical knowledge is invited to attend. These courses of lectures are often publicised by the road safety officer of the town or city concerned, and advertisements appear in local papers.

An incentive which has been offered occasionally to people who attend the whole series of lectures (usually four or five) is the opportunity to ride in a police patrol car which is actually on duty, as an unofficial observer. Such a ride can, in itself, be educational.

MASTER DRIVERS CLUB

Since there are still a few cars to be seen with this badge on them, this is included in this summary. Early in 1967 the British Safety Council announced from their headquarters at 163-173 Praed Street, London W2, that they had inaugurated the toughest test for British car drivers, comparable with the qualification of master mariner or master pilot. The scheme was favourably received by the press, and got off to a good start, being backed by Stirling Moss among other notable names. Unfortunately, however, the British public did not take to it, and it died a natural death.

CHAPTER EIGHT

Driving Abroad

The holidaymaker who undertakes a journey of any length outside his own country should consider carefully the terrain over which he will travel. The French Alps on the way to Monaco, for instance, are rather more demanding than a trip to Wales or Scotland.

The average driver contents himself with a study of foreign road signs, notes whether the natives customarily drive on the right- or left-hand side of the road, stains his headlamp lenses amber, and leaves it at that, having barely scratched the surface of the matter.

Let us consider the plan of action which should be adopted by the advanced driver.

First, the car receives a thorough servicing for the appropriate mileage it has covered to date. In addition, brakes are very thoroughly checked — by stripping and inspecting the shoes and linings, inspecting all metal and flexible hoses and renewing where there is the slightest room for doubt. Town and moderate country driving rarely provide one with an opportunity to sample the phenomenon termed 'brake fade', caused as a rule by brakes overheating on long downhill stretches. Repeated application causes heat to glaze the surfaces of the linings and renders them almost useless. In order to avoid this, first, have brakes in the best condition possible, and second, never descend long steep hills relying upon light brake pressure alone to control car speed. It is much better to change to a lower gear in plenty of time. When actually necessary to use the brakes, firm hard application is much better than half-hearted pressure which has to be maintained for a greater length of time, while, in the event of brakes becoming 'spongy', a series of quick firm jabs on the pedal (known as cadence braking) will usually remedy matters. Of course brakes should be evenly adjusted on all four wheels, or the car will pull to one side when you least want it to. When stopping in hilly country, it is unwise to rely on the handbrake alone to hold the car on a slope; leave it in bottom or reverse gear, with the wheels turned in towards the kerb for a downhill slope, or outwards on an uphill one. This provides three insurances against a runaway car.

In the UK the engines of most cars are rather drastically over-cooled for most of the year, but conditions are different elsewhere, and on mountainous roads it is common to experience overheating. This generally results in one of two things:

Gas-locking. This occurs if the petrol begins to vapourise as a reult of the unusual heat, and shows up in the petrol pump or the float chamber of the carburettor; it can even occur in the pipes, although this is fairly unusual. The result is an intermittent loss of power — the engine may stall completely — although if left for a few minutes it may be possible to restart normally. Solar radiation and the heat from the overworked engine combine to produce this effect. One remedy is to place a wet cloth on the petrol pump, and another on the carburettor. Re-wet the cloths every few miles, and the evaporation will probably assist in cooling the vital parts.

Boiling. Pulling a full load of passengers and luggage up hills is more than the normal engine is usually called upon to do, so it is not very surprising that there will be cooling problems. Also, water will boil at a lower temperature under the reduced pressure experience at higher altitudes. The radiator hoses will be under greater pressure for more of the time than they are normally, so, before starting out, have them checked and changed if necessary. A set of spare hoses is advisable, together with suitable clips, which are hard to obtain abroad. Should boiling occur, stop at once and open the bonnet in order to afford the engine an opportunity to cool off, because to proceed would mean loss of coolant and the possibility of a seized-up engine, or at the very least a blown cylinder-head gasket. It helps to have the heater on and the fan blowing at full blast; this will probably overheat you, but will help enormously to dissipate the heat generated by the engine.

Crossing the Irish Sea or the Channel may be achieved by air, hovercraft or car ferry. During the past couple of decades the choice of routes has increased considerably and you should shop around for the best compromise between comfort and cost. The AA and the RAC are both extremely helpful and, in addition to providing recommended routes, will advise on a host of likely queries. One point to remember is that if you wish to cross during the recognised holiday season, you will be wise to book your passage months in advance. The cross-Channel ferries provide a drive-on/drive-off facility, but at others you will, in all likelihood, have to watch your car driven onto a cargo net by somebody you have never seen before, and then hoisted in a manner which you consider most precarious and swung down into the depths of the ship's hold.

INSURANCE

Car. If you propose to use the services of the AA or the RAC it will certainly pay you to make use of their five star or *cordon bleu* travel plans. These provide a really worthwhile and very valuable type of insurance which can take care of almost

93

anything that may happen while you are away from home. Should you be camping, then tents and other equipment may be insured on the same plan as well as cover for the driver and passengers against possible medical treatment.

Although it is no longer essential for a motorist driving a British registered car to produce a 'green card' on entering either an EEC country or Austria, Czechoslovakia, East Germany (German Democratic Republic), Finland, Hungary, Norway, Sweden or Switzerland, it is still highly advisable to obtain one from your insurer. The green card is still internationally recognised evidence of insurance in the case of an accident. It will enable you to obtain readily and without further formality the benefit of the green card system of international claims' handling in respect of compulsory insurance claims. In addition, the only cover provided automatically in the above countries by the usual form of UK policy is limited to the requirements of the local compulsory insurance laws which may be very much less than the cover under your policy, so that when applying to your insurer for a green card you may ask to have your insurance extended to give full cover. The green card is also recognised in Bulgaria, Greece, Israel, Morocco, Poland, Portugal, Rumania, Spain, Tunisia, Turkey and Yugoslavia. Although your insurers may be able and willing to issue you with one for these countries, they may be unwilling to extend your full policy cover to apply in all of them. Should you forget to take a green card with you when travelling in these countries, you will be required to take out expensive short-term rates at the frontier of each country concerned in your itinerary.

If involved in an accident in any of the countries to which the green card applies, you should report it to the local motor insurers bureau whose address will be on the green card, unless you have been asked by your own insurer to report any accident to their own representative in that country.

When travelling to Spain, ask your insurer to issue a bail

bond which acts as a surety in the event of an accident, and may save your car or yourself from being impounded while the police carry out their investigations.

Many insurers issue policyholders with a standard form known as a European accident statement on notification that a vehicle is to be taken to Europe. Motorists involved in an accident abroad can record on the form the agreed facts about the accident without any admission of liability. The EAS is increasingly used in western Europe, and as the English translation follows the format of continental versions there should be no difficulty about agreeing the facts with other drivers who might be involved. Should you be unfortunate enough to have to use the form, send it to your own insurer together with the claim form.

Under a continental extension of your insurance cover, your car will normally be protected on journeys up to sixty-five hours on any of the recognised sea routes. Longer trips, or unusual routings, will of course require extra cover. If you are rich and decide to take your car by air, then insurance is normally included in the cost of the ticket; if not, contact your insurer.

Should you be really unlucky and have your car wrecked or stolen whilst abroad, you could be called upon to pay import duties, because foreign countries will regard your vehicle as an import if it is left there no matter what the reason may be. Of course your policy may cover this duty, but remember to check first. There are some insurers who also include the cost of redelivering your car to your home — but check this as well while you are at it. Better safe than sorry.

Enthusiastic caravanners who take their vans abroad will probably need extra cover, and an extra premium will usually secure this. In this event, however, make very sure that the caravan is included on the green card.

Note: A condition common to all holiday and travel insurance policies and to motor policies is the 'war risk' exclusion. This means that claims arising under any section of the policies and directly or indirectly caused by war or related risks will not be met by your insurers.

People. The wise man makes certain that he and his family are insured for cover against the need for medical treatment. The NHS does not operate abroad, although limited reciprocal arrangements are available in Common Market countries. In Austria, Bulgaria, the Channel Islands, Isle of Man, New Zealand, Norway, Poland, Sweden and Yugoslavia similar facilities are available, but in some cases only to a very limited extent. Medical benefits under these arrangements are generally available only on production of a certificate of entitlement (Form E111) obtainable from your local Department of Health and Social Security. Check the current benefits available at your local DHSS office. It is a regulation in most countries that you must disclose full details of any illness or condition of a permanent or recurring nature even though this information may not be specifically requested. The responsibility is yours.

You will need more cover for the United States or Canada, where medical treatment is even more expensive than on this side of the Atlantic. Broadly speaking, there are two main types of insurance for travellers abroad:

The Package Policy. This, for what it provides, is a very reasonable bargain. For around £2.50 to £3.00 you will be covered for a fortnight against the following: medical expenses up to about £1,000; cancellation of holiday due to accident, illness or jury service where a deposit is not recoverable, or by compulsory quarantine; luggage or articles which are lost or damaged and reported within twenty-four hours to the police, up to about £250; personal accident, death or permanent disablement up to around £1,000; and personal liability, which covers you against any injury or damage you may cause to others or their property up to nearly a quarter of a million pounds.

Selective Policies. These enable you to take out insurance for longer periods than under a package policy and to buy increased cover for some risks and ignore others if you wish. They enable you to choose exactly what you want, and can provide wider cover than the package policies.

CAMPING

Camp site operators and hoteliers often insist on retaining travellers' passports for the duration of their stay at the establishment. There is no need to be worried about this, but if you are perturbed about the possibility of loss, then obtain from the AA or RAC an international camping carnet. If you offer this instead of your passport it will be accepted. Such a document is usually provided as part of the five star or *cordon bleu* type of package deal. The ICC is also useful should you need to get the assistance of overseas motoring organisations.

Study guidebooks and maps which cover the country in which you will be driving, and if possible try to study some of the more relevant phrases in the appropriate language(s). If you make some effort to speak the language, however much you mutilate it, the nationals will usually appreciate that at least you are making an effort. The standard type of phrase-book isn't much use — petrol, for instance, goes by several names in Europe: *Benzin* in Germany and *essence* in France are common, but many forecourt assistants are equally familiar with petrol and gas. Make sure, though, that you actually get what you want. Paraffin instead of petrol would do your car no good at all.

The car log book, or its recent equivalent green form (Vehicle Registration Document V5) could save you embarrassing queries and wasted time, particularly if the car is fairly new.

Although relatively large sums may be easily and safely carried in the form of travellers' cheques (arranged through your bank) it is advisable to change some of them into the currency of the country you are in at the moment. When about to do so, first enquire from a reliable source what the current rate of exchange is at the time, and also what the service charge is for changing it. Some bureaux charge too much. On your return your bank will undoubtedly accept what notes or cheques you may have remaining but most banks boggle at accepting foreign coins. Lastly, ensure that before you go you know just how much you may legally take out of the country, since laws on this point vary from time to time.

It will assist the exchequer greatly if you can find room for a small stock of such things as your favourite brand of tea, or anything which you know is difficult to obtain abroad. Some countries impose regulations governing the quantity of foodstuffs you may import, but provided the amount in your hamper is obviously not intended for trading, most customs posts will turn a blind eye. They vary somewhat in their treatment of holidaymakers, but as long as you are patently honest and polite to them, they will almost certainly return the compliment.

As a general rule continental police will not permit overnight parking in laybys on main roads, but if you are well off the beaten track and exercise some discretion, nobody seems to worry unduly.

This is where the ICC can be useful once more; possession of one, although no longer required in Spain if camping on an official site, will usually enable one to camp on land other than that officially set aside for this purpose, although permission to camp should always be sought. A carnet is still needed for the state forests of France. This would not be valid in the USSR. *Gases for Camping and Caravanning.* Camping Gas International is available in the majority of countries throughout the world, but Calor Gas is available only in Great Britain, Northern Ireland and Eire, although it is known that there are certain isolated locations on the mainland where

Calor Gas bottles may be refilled. They are so few and far between that it is not safe to rely upon their existence when you need them.

DRIVING TECHNIQUES

The fact that to us the people of other countries we visit usually seem to be driving on the 'wrong' side of the road is usually a little disturbing at first, but, provided one is careful and concentrates for the first hour or so, there is nothing to be really worried about. Travellers' tales of breakneck speeds and a vast orchestra of horn-blowing are common, but there has been a growing tendency to drive in a somewhat more subdued manner for some time. Admittedly the continental driver is rather enthusiastic by nature, but he is also, as a rule, an excellent driver.

On the other hand, the driver abroad is not exactly what *we* would call 'polite'—if you leave the slightest gap he will immediately see that it is filled—hesitate at minor crossroads, and you will be in for a very long wait—sluggish getaways from lights mean a lively chorus of protesting horns, and so on. However, this is only a repetition of what one expects in some of our own large cities at the rush hour. If one drives positively and without hindering others, one will usually get on very well indeed. The horn is used much more than in Britain, for a toot is expected upon overtaking; if you forget to do so you will probably receive a protesting blast yourself!

Cruising speeds are often ignored outside towns, where the regulation speed should be religiously observed. Drivers abroad can show that they have patience, however, for on mountain roads they may be seen following a big diesel lorry quite happily at a mere 15-20 mph until a straight stretch enables them to pass safely.

Behaviour at crossroads or minor road junctions may at first appear well nigh suicidal to our insular eyes, but, providing one remembers the rule that drivers must give precedence to vehicles coming from the right, all should be well. Failure in this may result in serious accidents. It can seem quite alarming when a local driver shoots straight out into the traffic flow, but he knows the rules and is perfectly aware of what he is doing.

Apart from driving on the right and giving priority to vehicles joining the road from the right (except where you see the signs illustrated in Fig 10) in general traffic signs and laws

Figure 10   These signs all mean '*You* have priority', and are called 'Passage Protégé' signs: *top left*, yellow diamond with white border; *top right*, yellow triangle with 'crossroads' symbol (different to ours in that it is a diagonal cross); *centre*, yellow triangle with symbol for 'minor crossing'

are similar to those in the UK. Do, however, take extra care at roundabouts, where the regulations oblige you to give way to traffic entering it, and not to vehicles which are actually negotiating the one-way system.

White line markings similar to British ones are employed, and on three-lane roads the centre lane *really is* for overtaking only. The rules for pedestrian crossings are similar to those in the UK. Traffic lights, too, are similar, although there are often places where they may be suspended over the middle of the road, so watch for this.

Autoroutes, autobahns and autostrada have similar regulations to our motorways, but it is against the law for a pedestrian, even in the event of a breakdown, to walk to the nearest phone. He should wave down a passing vehicle and request the driver to report his situation. Most are very helpful and will often go out of their way to help a visitor.

Milestones and distance posts vary from country to country, but on the whole are reliable, always giving the distances between main cities accurate to the nearest kilometre, and often the distance to the next town.

Should you have an accident, stay in the car if possible. Try not to enter into any argument, no matter how incensed the other party may be. Leave the vehicles exactly as they are until the police arrive to measure skid marks and so on, and make any statement to them only.

The British tend to believe that they are the only people who normally drive on the left-hand side of the road, but in fact this is also the case in quite a number of other countries, such as Australia, many parts of Africa (with the exception of those which are or were colonies or protectorates of France, Belgium, Portugal and so on), Ceylon, Burmah, Fiji, India, Hong Kong, Malaya, Mauritius, New Zealand, Pakistan, Singapore and some others. In many it is what amounts to a kind of free for all, with lorries driving down the middle of the road in order to avoid bullock carts and camels. If you are planning to visit a completely strange country, then consult the AA or RAC, who will be pleased to advise you of any unusual traffic regulations and customs.

Another point upon which the average British car differs

101

from those generally found abroad is that the British driver is usually content with an interior mirror unless he is accustomed to towing. This isn't much use when driving on the right-hand side of the road, so in order to be prepared for both types of driving, it is perhaps best to have wing mirrors fitted.[4]

Drivers in other countries are fairly intolerant of whitish headlamps, and prefer amber lights; in fact many continental countries make it illegal to show white lights, since they claim that they are more likely to dazzle oncoming traffic. There are two methods available for curing this; painting the lenses with a special compound which is easily removed later by a rag soaked in petrol, or replacing the lamps with a type designed especially for the country you are about to visit. The latter is the more expensive method, but perhaps the most satisfactory if your trip is going to be a reasonably extensive one. With an older car (prior to sealed-beam headlamps) you can change the bulbs for the amber type. Changing the lamps is best, for they will then dip in the required direction. This expense, however, may be avoided by fixing amber discs, which deflect the beam, over existing headlamps.

As already mentioned, heat in some countries is much more of a problem than in Britain, so that in the middle of the day tyres are subjected to greater stresses. The wise driver frequently checks pressures, removes flints which lodge in the treads, and makes a habit of parking in the shade whenever possible — if there is little or no shade, hang something like a piece of sacking where it can cast some shade on the poor long-suffering wheels. Batteries, too, suffer in excessive heat and electrolyte evaporates at an unexpected rate, so regular checks are necessary. Wicker-work back-rests are worthwhile considering if you would avoid the unpleasant feeling of your shirt sticking to your back, and sunglasses are, to some people, a necessity.

In cities where there are tramlines, like Genoa, watch for cobbles, for they are rather dicey when the road is wet, and when driving on some of the more mountainous roads look out for a white triangle with a red border carrying a vertical black line. This means falling stones are a local hazard, though what one is supposed to do about it I can't say.

Lastly, there is no need whatever to clutter up stowage space with excess spares. Take a spare fanbelt, hoses, points and plugs to suit your car; the rest can be purchased locally as and when required. Don't forget the red warning triangle in case of a breakdown, though, because in most countries today they are obligatory.

CHAPTER NINE

An Introduction to Motor Sport

The first international governing body of motor sport, the *Alliance Internationale des Automobile Clubs Reconnus* (AIACR) was established in 1904 and reconstituted in 1946 as the *Fédération Internationale de L'automobile*. In Britain the Royal Automobile Club (originally the Automobile Club of Great Britain and Ireland) was founded in 1897 and granted the prefix 'Royal' by His Majesty King Edward VII in 1907. The RAC is the British governing body of motor sport, and the FIA's representative in Britain.

Today motor sport takes many forms: sprints, hillclimbs, rallies, autocross, road and track racing, dragster racing and straightforward record breaking. If you fancy having a go yourself, the most appropriate branch of motor sport for you will depend upon two factors:

1 your own natural aptitude and personal skill;
2 the complacency of your bank manager.

However, no matter which branch of the sport you desire to participate in, you will certainly require the following documents, available from the Motor Sport Division of the RAC, 31 Belgrave Square, London SW1.

Competition Licence. This is renewable annually, and issued

Figure 11   The holder of a Competition Licence is entitled to this windscreen sticker, in red, white and blue, issued by the RAC

to cover restricted, national and international events. When you have completed at least six events successfully in your chosen sport in closed or restricted competitions (for which your licence is originally valid) you may apply for upgrading to national status. Similarly, completion of six nationals will qualify you for upgrading to international status and put you among the veterans.

Record Card. Details of your performances in the lower grades will be inserted on this and countersigned by the clerk of the course. This document has to be forwarded to the RAC with your application for upgrading.

Medical Certificate. This card may be signed by your own doctor at the time he checks your general health and eyesight. It must be produced at every meeting you attend as a competitor.

You would also be well advised to purchase the current RAC *Motor Sport Year Book and Fixture List.* This contains the regulations for the organisation of motor competitions, and also lists such things as all motor clubs recognised by the RAC, together with the names and addresses of their secretaries, locations and maps of major British circuits, RAC appointed scrutineers, timekeepers and so on. It also contains a wealth of information about specials, GTs and sports cars, 'inexpensive' motor racing, rallying and so forth.

There is one type of competition not specifically mentioned above, and that is the driving test such as the RAC 'L Driver of the Year', based primarily upon skill and accuracy in handling a car against the clock.

It is advisable first to join a local car club, for their members are all keen drivers who continually strive to improve their driving techniques. Here you will acquire a great deal of motoring know-how, and be able to enter the competitions which they regularly organise. When you are able to acquit yourself fairly well in these you can graduate to the treasure hunt and rally.

Obviously your vehicle will require vastly different preparation for, say, a club treasure hunt and a ten thousand mile marathon rally, and so will the quantity and quality of spares you will carry. A local club event may call for nothing more elaborate than a spare tyre, fanbelt and maybe plugs and points, whereas preparation for a really tough rally could be undertaken only by one of the major motor manufacturers.

Quite a number of reputable firms make it their business to specialise in producing do-it-yourself tuning kits, and these range from the simplest to the most elaborate, and include such exotica as high compression heads, special valve springs, manifolds, carburettors, competition clutches and so on. In addition they offer special parts for brakes, steering, suspension, etc. However, if you are not mechanically minded, it is better to have your car tuned by a specialist garage.

Quite a lot of people start with saloon car racing and here there are a lot of things which should be removed from the vehicle. Rip out all the carpeting, extra seats, internal trim and other unnecessary junk. This could make a difference of quite a few knots when getting away from the starting line. Basically only three instruments are essential to the role of the saloon racer—tachometer, oil pressure gauge, and water temperature gauge. Get instruments with large dials for good visibility, and borrow your wife's or girlfriend's nail varnish to mark clearly the spot on the dial where each needle will be under ideal running conditions so that you won't have to peer at it when lapping quickly. Train yourself to keep a weather eye on these gauges, as any divergence from normal at speed will mean an essential pit stop just as soon as you can possibly manage it.

You would be well advised to fit a 'full harness' type of seat belt rather than the 'lap only' type which unfortunately, one sees so often in road cars. A fire extinguisher (powder type) should be securely fixed within easy reach, and the ignition key clearly ringed with vivid red paint—in the event of trouble a marshall may want to get at it swiftly. Fireproof, or, flameproof, overalls are a sound investment together with a crash helmet.

When your car is ready, the clever thing to do is to try it out on a real circuit under racing conditions as near to the actual thing as possible. Your best step is to book a private practice session at one of the three main schools for racing drivers:

Motor Racing Stables, Brands Hatch Circuit, Fowkham, Nr Dartford, Kent;

Jim Russell Racing Drivers' School, Downham Market, Norfolk;

The Lydden Racing School, 2 London Road, Sittingbourne, Kent.

If you can persuade your mechanic to come along with you then, at the same time, he can fix anything that needs a little twiddling.

For rallying it is really a matter of putting things on rather than taking them off, because it isn't your all-out top speed which is the vital factor. Here we concentrate mainly on acceleration, handling and braking. Comfort and ease in handling maps, route cards and so on will also be greatly appreciated by your co-driver. Make sure he has plenty of room, for he will have to contend with several maps and many other documents on a long rally.

You'll probably also need some Koni shock absorbers, servo assisted brakes, rally-type seats and quartz halogen spotlights. Don't forget your navigator's reading light, which should be of the kind that doesn't shine in either his or the driver's eyes.

To a racing driver motor racing isn't really as dangerous as it appears to the layman. On the track the driver is racing against people who are at least as reliable as himself. Their skill has to be reasonably comparable or there would be no competition, and they are all circulating in the same direction, albeit rather quickly.

The origins of the RAC are as colourful as one would expect, despite its rather formal background in Pall Mall. Back in 1897, on a freezing winter morning, a group of 120 pioneers of motoring met at premises off Whitehall and founded the Automobile Club of Great Britain and Ireland. Its first functions were to furnish members with lists of places where oil, petrol, water and so forth were available, and where they could perhaps have their batteries charged. The first secretary, Mr Claude Johnson, arranged an exhibition to popularise the new form of transport, and only two years after the formation of the club Britain was treated to its first motor show. This turned out to be a week's gymkhana at the Old Deer Park at Richmond, where there was a grandstand capable of holding over 600 people. This overlooked a cinder track measuring more than a third of a mile around. One of the most important competitions was to be a race between one of the new horseless carriages and a horse called Gold Ring pulling a racing sulky. Gold Ring behaved impeccably until they started up the engine of the new machine when he immediately took off into the blue, and the race was temporarily postponed. Meanwhile two of the early 'star' names, S. F. Edge and Charles Jarrott raced each other round the track on de Dion tricycles.[5] This was followed by a demonstration of driving skill during which the competitors had to negotiate a winding path between wands and finish with a reversing operation. Later there were further demonstrations which involved the driver climbing out on to the footboard of the vehicle and leaning far over to pick up objects such as handkerchiefs as he hurtled past them at speeds hitherto undreamed of. In the course of this one driver actually tumbled out of his car, but, fortunately, was able to run after it and climb back aboard before it had done more than demolish one of the marker wands. By this time Gold Ring had been caught and led back to the starting post. This time he behaved with decorum. The race got off to a good start and he ran well. Perhaps too well, for he soundly beat a Barriere motor tricycle by about half a lap. The famous S. F. Edge was therefore recalled with his de Dion to compete against the horse-drawn sulky, and this time the 'car' won, although obviously because Gold Ring's driver had misunderstood his instructions and pulled up a little too soon.

Staging this show had cost the new club an immense amount of money for those days, as a result of which its bank balance was in a precarious state. It was decided, therefore, to enrol life members at £25 each, which expedient averted a financial crisis. His Majesty King Edward VII was the first royal motorist, and approved the club's badge for members. The badge usually seen on the average family car is the badge to which an associate member is entitled.

As well as in the Grand Prix and Tourist Trophy races, the British International Rally, the British Trials Championship and the annual veteran car run from London to Brighton, the RAC awards titles to the foremost driver in saloon car and sports car racing, hillclimbs, rallies, autocross and driving tests.

For driving test competitions many types of car are eminently suitable. Ideal are the popular sports cars such as

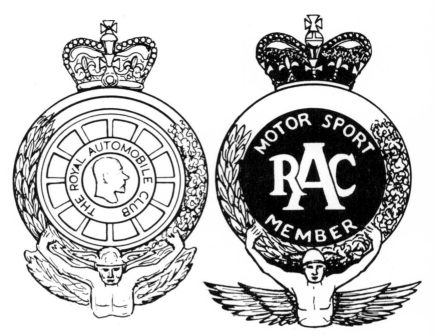

Figure 12   RAC car badges available to members: *left,* full membership badge (showing head of King Edward VIII); *right,* Competition Licence Holder's badge (the badge usually seen on the average family car is the badge to which an Associate Member is entitled)

the MGB and its derivatives, the Midget and the MGB GT, to say nothing of the Sunbeams, Minis, Morgans, Datsuns, Imps, Hondas and SAABs. The MGB is a particularly 'forgiving' car. It handles extremely well and has acquired a high degree of popularity. Most of the expensive cars will, if well driven, beat it in dry conditions, but when the ground is wet or slippery the MG begins to show its paces.

The diagrams for some tests (see Fig 3) may, at first glance look as mysterious as the electrical wiring circuits of the car itself, involving, as they do, lots of standing and flying starts, backing and filling over lines marked A, B, C and sometimes even P and Q. Careful examination will soon reveal, however, just what the compiler had in mind. Normally driving tests are carried out on fairly level ground which isn't likely to damage your car, except for the backing and filling over white lines, where you have to stop quickly, then reverse and maybe go ahead again and stop over another line, take off again and finish astride yet another. In such a test, unless you time things perfectly, your gearbox and/or clutch could take a real beating. Remember that quite a standard car can win these tests, if it is better driven than the others. Before going in for any test, study the diagram for it carefully and be absolutely certain of what is required before going up to the line.

Points to look for before commencing any section of a test are:

1 type of test start, ie flag, word of marshall, electronic device, also is it a standing or flying start? Don't forget that from a standing start you are usually allowed to engage first gear and wait with clutch disengaged and handbrake on. A fly-off type of handbrake can be helpful;

2 what is the actual purpose of this particular test? Make sure you know *exactly* where your car has to go, precisely where it has to stop, restart, reverse and so on. Make sure you know the meaning of every marker;

3 type of finish, ie flying finish, stop beyond line, or astride line, etc. Remember to apply the handbrake when the car comes to a halt.

It will pay you to study the system of marking before attempting any test, in order to decide whether to concentrate on accuracy or timing.

Notice that in the tests suggested in Chapter Two competitors can lose 10 points for each time they have to restart their engines, and no less than 50 points each time they forget the handbrake. Have your car really comfortable; the handbrake, gearlever and so on must almost fall into your hand when you are sitting naturally. It is little things like this which win events and get competitors into national finals.

When you begin to enter really tough driving tests you will find that a useful art to master is the handbrake turn. It is fairly simple to execute, but should first be practised on *deserted* land. Position your hands ready to take a whacking great handful of wheel, then, at a reasonable speed, swing your wheel hard over, disengage the clutch and yank on the handbrake hard at the same time. This starts a spin and, by controlling the initial speed into the turn and the amount of handbrake pressure applied, together with the precise moment of release, you can decide for yourself whether the spin will be a vicious one. Just as the car is coming onto the correct heading, you drop the handbrake, engage clutch and accelerate. If you begin with practice at reasonable speeds you can gradually speed things up a little at each subsequent attempt. Handbrake turns are most useful when one has to spin the car fairly rapidly in a test which necessitates going into and out of 'garages' quickly, or perhaps turning around a pylon well away from the rest of the test.

Autocross is another motor sport designed to afford you fiendish pleasure of a high order, and rallycross is perhaps even more thrilling.

By the mid-fifties 'cross events were becoming really organised, and soon John Player & Sons became involved as sponsors. Commercialism then of course began to attract the semi-professional driver. 'Cross almost immediately developed into an organised sport in its own right, and competition at a national level followed as a matter of course, each Sunday between spring and autumn, finding events scheduled, while national events gather crowds from far and near.

Generally cars compete in pairs over a course at least 30ft wide and 600yd long, and when the first pair have negotiated a little over half the course a second pair may be started. Given a sufficiently large course, even a third pair may be sent away once the second pair is well clear.

The classes which are now recognised are listed, among other things, in the RAC *Motor Sport Year Book*. Stipulations are incorporated in the rules regarding clothing, crash helmets and spectator safety, and also fire and medical provisions. Fortunately when the flag drops, the drivers themselves don't have too many rules and regulations to worry about beyond keeping all four wheels actually inside the boundaries of the track, and avoiding entanglement with marker posts. (Each one of these pranged means a five-second penalty.)

Before having a bash at this, make sure you are really good on wet and dry grass — also on dust and mud. Compared with racetracks, speeds are relatively slow, but like all other things in this world that is a relative statement.

It was ITV which really boosted rallycross, originating it specially for television early in 1967. Autocross and rallycross are basically fairly similar sports, the main differences being in the nature and layout of the courses and starting arrangements. In rallycross the course is wickedly crooked and includes grass, tarmac, gravel, loose and packed, sand, mud, bumps, inclines, watersplashes and any other devilish devices the organisers can find to make it 'interesting'. As the RAC puts it, the course is laid out on 'a combination of sealed and unsealed surfaces'. In order to make things look more exciting on the TV screen they start cars four at a time. There are even fewer rules and regulations than in autocross, and up till now no separate categories have been laid down by the 'powers that be'.

Cars take off, perform some, perhaps unscheduled, aerobatics, then make a dicey landing and shoot off in hot pursuit of a rival who, through good luck or good judgement, made a slightly better landing or got away better. So much mud is shipped by the cars that it entails cutting a slit through the windscreen for the driver to peer through; this is called the 'letterbox look'. The primary interest while driving any 'cross car is to keep it going as hard as possible in order to put up the best time which is not exactly the easiest thing in the world to do when most of your wheels are off the ground for most of the time. In fact for many seconds at a time you may not even be heading in the correct direction, and it is sometimes quite an achievement to keep the vehicle upright. New situations materialise and have to be met with lightning reactions, equalled only by rallying proper. Even in full-blooded rally conditions, though, situations seldom change quite so often and so suddenly in such a short interval of time.

Naturally all this means a great deal more than just banging your boot to the floor and hoping for the best. Often the margin between a correctly negotiated bend and completely losing the road in an uncontrolled slide is very narrow indeed. Hence the need for safety belts, roll-over bars and so on.

'Cross sports are both very fair and very tough indeed, and are certainly not for gentle drivers.

One would imagine that because specials are built for the job they would have a better chance than standard cars, but this is by no means the case as a good car without a good driver is next to useless. So far as the car itself is concerned, what you need most of all is lots of bottom-end power to reduce gear-changing and provide lots of traction. Jettison all unnecessary weight, just as in saloon car racing.

Should you eventually decide to go in for 'cross motoring, then you'll find you can be pretty busy throughout the year. The sport is rapidly catching on on the continent, and with the EEC conditions more cash is being attracted to meetings. There is absolutely no doubt that its popularity is soaring despite the fact that the pound, which would almost fill the average tank when I started, now buys little more than a gallon.

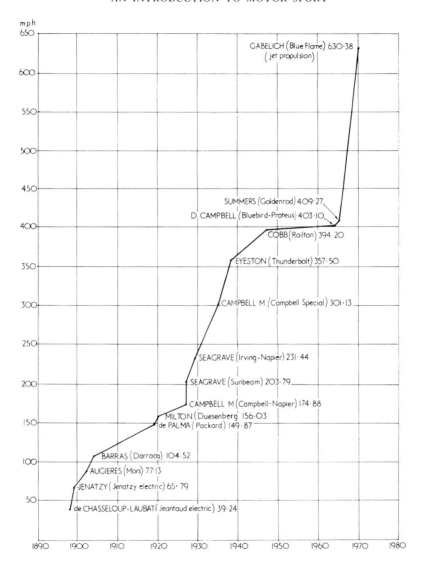

Figure 13   World speed records 1890-1977

115

CHAPTER TEN

Qualifications for Driving Instructors

There is a rather hackneyed saying which states 'Those who can, do; those who can't, teach'. In the field of driving instruction this is manifestly untrue, for a poor driver will inevitably pass on his faults to his pupils. Anyone who aspires to become a professional instructor must have several good qualities, but perhaps the two main desirables are extreme patience and a sense of dedication. It goes without saying that he should be prepared to work hours which no trade union would countenance for a moment, because he has to arrange his tuition timing to coincide with his pupils' available hours. He should also be of impeccable character, reasonably smart and very methodical.

For the past few years it has been illegal to give driving instruction for reward in cash or kind unless qualified to do so by having passed the Department of Transport's test for approved driving instructors, provided the required references, and been placed upon the official register. Prior to this anybody and everybody could take up instruction as a sort of part-time pin-money hobby, provided they held a full driving licence. It is nevertheless a fact that there are still occasional unqualified people who are battening upon the gullibility of the unfortunate public. Where the authorities become aware of this, they will prosecute, but the law is rather difficult to enforce in this respect for, obviously, an offender must be caught in the act. The fact that there is nothing whatever against teaching a friend or relative, provided no money or other consideration passes, means that ordinary L-plates are unlikely to stimulate suspicion, and so the charlatans are able to operate undetected and remain undiscouraged by any form of effective deterrent. The insurance companies could assist by denying cover to people who provide unauthorised tuition, perhaps, but certainly the law, if it is not to be brought into disrepute, should be tightened up in such a manner as to preclude imposters.

The genuinely qualified instructor who is dedicated to his work will obtain all the qualifications possible in his field.

The legal minimum qualification is the Department of Transport's approval, and people granted this are expected to display the certificate issued to them in a prominent position inside the vehicle used for tuition. Other qualifications are registration with the driving instruction department of the Royal Automobile Club and/or the Motor Schools Association. Of them all, the RAC is undoubtedly the most helpful to the instructors on its register. Over the past twelve years the Ministry of Transport (before it became the DoT) issued a bulletin to approved driving instructors in November 1965, and made two issues of leaflets entitled *ADI News* in April 1968 and October 1969; apart from these they have, to the best of my knowledge, offered no help whatever to approved instructors beyond the six-monthly visit from their area supervising examiner when an instructor is checked for his continuing efficiency, attitude to the pupil and so on. This leaves little time for discussion. It is also seldom carried out with any degree of regularity.

The RAC Instructors' Register, on the other hand, issues a

monthly *Members' News* and a regular printed newspaper called *The Instructor*, besides notifying all on their register of any impending changes in the laws, rules, regulations, signs and other developments concerned with motoring. They are also extremely helpful in the event of instructors raising queries, not only about the technicalities of their profession, but also concerning the running of driving schools, insurance, advertising and many other points.

The Motor Schools Association also issue periodical information to their members. The person holding any of these qualifications is entitled to display the special L-plates which are of a design acceptable to the authority concerned. This can result in a multiplicity of plates on school cars which are sometimes, perhaps, confusing to would-be pupils. It is sufficient to remember that all genuine instructors have to hold the minimum qualification, so that really the DoT plates are unnecessary if either the RAC or MSA plates are carried on the car. Several plates fore and aft serve only to make the car look a mess, and impress nobody. Also, now that the law has changed to permit the L on the roof sign to be regarded as the obligatory one on the car, small insignia on the car roof sign are much neater and cost less anyway.

Dual Controls. Instruction may, of course, be given in cars where these are not fitted, provided the handbrake, ignition key and steering wheel are easily accessible to the instructor. I would, however, hesitate to rely on a handbrake alone to stop a car in an emergency, and strongly recommend the fitting of properly designed duals. These are of two main types — cable operated and bar operated. Of the two, the latter is more positive in action and requires less maintenance. Normally only the footbrake and clutch are covered by the operating arms, although it is possible to have accelerator control in addition. If this is done, however, there is a requirement that it be disconnected for each driving test on which the car is to be used. Examiners are not permitted to conduct a test in a car in which the accelerator is dual controlled.

THE DEPARTMENT OF TRANSPORT

This is the minimum legal requirement for a professional driving instructor since registration became compulsory on 1 October 1970, when the trainee licensing scheme was also introduced. The present governing legislation is Part V of the Road Traffic Act 1972 read in conjunction with the following Regulations: 1968 — nos 84, 85, 86, 713; 1970 — 965, 966, 967; 1971 — 351; 1973 — 2013; 1976 — 1077.

There are at present just over 20,000 registered instructors under the scheme.

The DoT state that their last news bulletin was issued to instructors in 1969 because it became impossible to continue sending newsletters to all the individual instructors, but in any case their value was considerably diminished by publication of the department's manual *Driving*. Approved driving instructors can get comprehensive information about all driving techniques from this manual, and the local supervising examiner (ADI) will help as required on instructional matters.

A proposal to introduce written tests as part of the DoT test received no general support from the motoring organisations, and was therefore abandoned.

Application forms for registration, or for the granting of a licence for a trainee instructor may be obtained from any of the department's traffic area offices, and these are also the offices to which application for driving tests are sent.

Qualifications. Anyone who wishes to become an approved driving instructor must:

1 have held a full driving licence for at least four years;

2 not have been under a disqualification for driving for any part of the four years preceding the application;

3 be a fit and proper person to have his name entered upon the register;

4 pass the register qualifying examination.

The examination for entry to the register consists of both a written and practical part, and the applicant must pass the written part first before being allowed to take the practical part. Should he fail the practical and not be able to pass it within three years, he must take the written part again. The latter may be taken at any of the larger towns in the UK, and the applicant may decide for himself at which test centre he wishes to be examined.

The Written Part. This part of the examination consists of three question papers; 1 hour 20 minutes is allowed for the completion of the first and second papers together, and a further 1 hour 20 minutes for the third paper. Questions will be on all or any of the following subjects:

1 the principles of road safety generally and their application in particular circumstances;

2 the techniques of driving a car correctly, courteously and safely, including control of the vehicle; road procedure; recognising hazards and taking proper action; dealing properly with pedestrians and other road users; the use of safety equipment;

3 the tuition required to instruct a pupil in driving a car, including the items in 2 above; the correction of the pupil's errors; the manner of the instructor; the relationship between instructor and pupil, and simple vehicle adaptations for disabled drivers;

4 the *Highway Code* and other matters in the booklet in which it is published;

5 the DL68 (your driving test);

6 the interpretation of the 'reasons for failure' given in the DL24 (the statement of failure to pass the driving test);

7 knowledge, adequate to the needs of driving instruction, of the mechanism and design of a car;

8 the book *Driving* — the official manual issued by the Department of Transport and published by HM Stationery Office.

The Practical Part. This consists of tests of eyesight, driving technique and instructional ability. It lasts altogether about two hours, and a candidate must pass all three of its parts on one and the same occasion.

Eyesight. For this the requirement is to read a car numberplate at a distance of 90ft where the letters are 3⅛in high (100ft for the older 3½in symbols) in good daylight and with the aid of spectacles if worn. Failure in this means the test is terminated.

Driving Technique. This follows the lines of the learner driver test, but a higher standard of competence is expected. The candidate must satisfy the examiner that he has an adequate knowledge of the principles of good driving and road safety and that he can apply them in practice. In particular he must satisfy the examiner in all or any of the following:

1 his expert handling of the controls;

2 his correct use of road procedure;

3 his anticipation of the actions of other road users and the taking of appropriate action;

4 his sound judgment of distance, speed and timing;

5 his consideration for the convenience and safety of other road users. He must also show his ability to perform all or any of the following:

1 move away straight ahead or at an angle;

2 overtake, meet or cross the path of other vehicles and take an appropriate course;

3 turn right-hand and left-hand corners correctly;

4 stop the vehicle in an emergency;

5 drive the vehicle backwards, and while doing so enter limited openings to the right and to the left;

6 cause the vehicle to face in the opposite direction by the use of forward and reverse gears.

The routes used include roads, both in built-up areas and outside them which carry considerable traffic, and the applicant will be expected to make reasonable use of the performance potential of the vehicle with safety.

Instructional Ability. The candidate will be expected to show his knowledge and ability by giving practical instruction to the examiner acting as the pupil, assuming the examiner to be, successively, an absolute beginner, a learner driver with some knowledge, and one who is about to take the driving test of the DoT. For each of these three phases the examiner will nominate one or more of the following as the basis of the instruction in which he wishes to examine the candidate:

1 explanation of the car's controls;

2 moving off and making normal progress;

3 driving the vehicle backwards, and while doing so entering limited openings to the right and/or left;

4 turning the vehicle round on the road to face in the opposite direction by the use of the forward and reverse gears;

5 parking close to the kerb, using reverse gear;

6 using the mirror and explaining how to make an emergency stop;

7 approaching corners;

8 judgment of speed and general road positioning;

9 dealing with road junctions;

10 meeting, crossing the path of and overtaking other vehicles;

11 allowing adequate clearance to other road users and dealing with pedestrian crossings.

Assessment will be made on the method, clarity, adequacy and correctness of the instruction given by the candidate, the observation and correction of driving errors committed by the 'pupil', and the candidate's general manner.

The arrangement of suitable insurance to cover car, candidate and examiner during the test is the responsibility of the candidate, who should provide the car. This should be a suitable saloon or estate car in proper condition and capable of normal performance for vehicles of its type. It should have a non-automatic transmission system, right-hand steering, a readily adjustable driving seat and a seat for a forward-facing passenger. The candidate should also provide two L-plates with provision for attachment to the car when required.

Once he or she has passed both parts of the test, an instructor is then eligible for registration which, in the first instance, lasts for four years, at the end of which period it may be renewed upon application and payment of the appropriate fee for further periods of four years at a time. The fee for the written part of the examination is £15, and successful candidates are then required to pay a further fee of £25 before taking the practical part. On passing both, registration is free for the first four years. Renewal of registration costs £25. The fee payable for a combined trainee instructor's licence and admission to the written part of the examination is £30. A trainee's licence alone is £15.

When renewing one's registration it is not necessary to take the qualifying examination again unless there has been a lapse of a year or more since the expiry of the last period of registration.

Upon registration, an instructor is entitled to designate himself a Department of Transport approved driving instructor (DOTADI), and he then receives an official certificate of registration which incorporates his name, photograph and official title. The certificate is designed to be suitable for display in the car normally used for tuition. Should an instructor lose or accidentally destroy his certificate, he can usually obtain a duplicate on payment of 50p.

The address to which all enquiries or applications should be sent is the same as that to which an ordinary DoT L test application should be sent, ie one's own traffic area office of the DoT, but any information they may be unable to supply can be obtained from:

The Department of Transport
2 Marsham Street
London SW1P 3EB

(For the written part of the examination, take a set of drawing instruments and a few coloured pencils, so that suitable diagrams may be drawn to illustrate your answers. For the practical part, have car and self immaculate.)

THE ROYAL AUTOMOBILE CLUB

In an attempt to reduce the number of road accidents, many of which were directly attributable to lack of proper instruction, the RAC instituted in 1935 an examination and a voluntary system of certification and registration of driving instructors.

Driving instruction acquired a new importance with the introduction of the compulsory Ministry of Transport driving test that same year, and the RAC felt the time was appropriate for the elevation of the status of instructors, with corresponding advantage to the pupil and an increase in general road safety. The object of registration is to ensure that driving instructors are properly qualified for the profession by investigating their background fairly thoroughly.

Although it will soon be half a century since the examination was first conducted, continual changes are being made in order to keep the methods in line with modern development and conditions. Special attention is paid to the assessment of candidates' ability to teach a pupil up to the required standard in the shortest possible time. Question papers are altered from time to time in order to include recent legislation, and the practical test is a realistic one, the candidate instructing a genuine novice (provided by the club) in the presence of an examiner.

In order that a pupil may be in no doubt that he or she is actually receiving instruction from a registered instructor, all who successfully pass the rather stringent examination are issued with a certificate in the form of a small identity card bearing the holder's photograph, which should be affixed to the facia panel of the school car when instruction is being given.

New terms and gradings for RAC registration came into force on 1 January 1977. Before decimalisation of currency in 1971 an RAC registered instructor who was a full member of the now-defunct Institute of RACRIs paid one basic fee to cover RAC registration plus all the extra information services institute membership brought, which included regular issues of the *Instructor* and *Members News*, with access to the full range of RAC registered driving instructors' publicity and training aids. All these services have since been continued and have been given to *all* RACRIs solely on payment of the annual re-registration fee, itself unchanged, apart from the addition of VAT, since then. Since this has turned into an increasingly uneconomic situation due to soaring costs, the RAC instructor's re-registration fee has now been increased to £6, and renewal is due on the anniversary of each original registration. Every RACRI receives a renewal notice sufficiently early to complete renewal by his or her due date. From 1 January 1977 the examination fee for intending new RACRIs is £10; this includes, if successful, a full ensuing year's RAC registration. The reasonableness of the fee and the services provided should be no deterrent to those DOTADIs who wish to earn a second qualification and display the club's imprimateur.

There is also a new category of driving school. It used to be that schools who were staffed exclusively by RACRIs, had suitable premises, and were of high repute, could apply for RAC registration. Now well run schools which take into account the growth of classroom driver education may apply for registration as RAC registered driver training centres. At all of these the intention is that not only should the greater part of the instruction be given by RACRIs, but that the business side also should be organised and run at an efficient and acceptable level. This means that to be an RAC registered school, whether having one instructor or twenty, more than half of those teaching must be RACRIs, there must be a room set aside for full-time use as a driving school office with proper facilities for business correspondence, with approved training and progress records for pupils, and during normal business hours there must be a telephone which is either fully manned or automatically records, with a satisfactory system for dealing with incoming calls.

An RAC registered driver training centre goes somewhat further, needing at least two RACRIs. It also needs satisfactory location and external appearance, an adequate, well decorated reception room, approved facilities for indoor instruction on road safety subjects and a receptionist on duty during business hours.

There are fees for initial inspection and registration and annual re-registration of these establishments, but so far as existing RAC registered schools are concerned, they are still welcome to continue for the present under the RAC registered school title on payment of the appropriate fee, unless and until they wish to be regraded.

Complete details of regrading etc may be obtained from the Register of RAC Driving Schools, RAC House, Lansdowne Road, Croydon CR9 2JA, as may full names and addresses of local RAC registered instructors, driving schools and driver training centres.

To be eligible for RAC registration an instructor must:

1 be twenty-one years of age or over;

2 have an impeccable personal reputation and driving history;

3 have held a full British licence to drive a car for at least four years;

4 have passed the examination for RAC registration.

Persons of both sexes may be registered.

In addition to the car certificate, a diploma is issued to successful candidates; this remains the property of the club.

Applicants for registration should submit the official form, supplied on request, together with the initial fee; two statements as to reputation signed by persons of standing, eg magistrates, police officers, solicitors, bank managers, notaries public, etc, and a personal declaration signed by the candidate in the presence of another householder. Disclosures made in personal declarations will be considered on their merits and the club may make such further enquiries as it thinks fit. Appointment for examination is made only after satisfactory completion of character references.

The examination consists of:

The Practical Test. This is conducted with a pupil supplied by the RAC, and is designed to reveal the extent of the candidate's driving and teaching ability, knowledge of driving requirements in the UK, and the working of a motor vehicle from the driver's viewpoint. An examiner will sit in the back of the car during the test, and will state exactly what he requires the candidate to do or teach.

The Written Test. For persons who are not already Department of Transport approved driving instructors, this test lasts approximately three hours. There are usually eight questions on the *Highway Code*, DL68 and other knowledge required for the standard of instruction required in Britain.

Should a candidate fail either the practical or written part of the examination, he or she will, upon further application and payment of the appropriate fee, be re-examined only in the part failed. The club reserves the right to decide the period which shall elapse before re-examination.

To use the name or symbol of the RAC in connection with any business or profession is permitted only under a special licence from the club. Registered instructors may, of course, use the words 'RAC Registered Instructor' after their names, but all prospectuses, advertisements, and printing matter in which reference is made to the club qualification of a registered instructor, and for which he or his employer is directly responsible, must be submitted to the club in duplicate and be approved before publication. It is important

127

to note that approval constitutes a licence only for the matter submitted.

The above extracts are the most important ones applying to aspiring candidates for registration; the full rules and regulations are supplied when application for registration is made.

For the practical test, a candidate should use his own car, or a school car to which he is accustomed, but, in any case, L-plates should be displayed, and there should be either dual controls fitted, or a central handbrake.

There are no 'catch' questions whatever in either part of the examination, but a candidate should be prepared for apparently silly questions from the pupil in the practical part, and answer them if possible with sketches where applicable. For the written part, take with you compasses, ruler and coloured pencils, so that you can produce clear and meaningful sketches to illustrate your answers. Don't assume knowledge on the part of the examiners—explain as fully as you can. After all, three hours for eight questions is quite generous.

THE MOTOR SCHOOLS ASSOCIATION OF GREAT BRITAIN LIMITED

Founded on 31 March 1935 by and for driving instructors, and governed by them. Since the vast majority of professional instructors trade under the name of 'driving school' or 'school of motoring', the association's name was appropriately chosen. The MSA embraces under its title every section of the profession, having members in Great Britain, Ireland, the Isle of Man and the Channel Islands.

By the will of the members there are three categories of membership:

1 'school'—two cars or more—present fee £14 per annum;

2 'self-employed'—one-car schools—present fee £9 per annum;

3 'employee' — works for others — present fee £5 per annum.

The scheme covers some 4,500 approved driving instructors, including roughly 1,300 in the first two categories. Many employees are 'covered' by the membership of their employer.

The MSA used to examine instructors, and had a register of approximately 4,000 when they closed it in favour of the Ministry of Transport scheme in 1967. Members may still, however, take it voluntarily.

The basic requirement to join the MSA is now to hold a DoT certificate of approval as a driving instructor.

The association offers training facilities for driving school staff, including basic ADI courses, driving school management courses and a staff instructor's course (for those giving internal training in their schools — as owners, managers or staff instructors). There is also an engineering division, mainly advisory, but involved in trying out various training aids for use in the car and other relevant investigations. There are also facilities for members, through this division, for the supply of batteries, oil, tyres and so on.

The Applied Psychological Research Unit is at the moment busy on a variety of subjects, the main one being the fact that drivers do not seem to be able to 'see' motorcyclists.

A bi-monthly newspaper *The MSA News* is issued to members; it deals with a large variety of diverse problems of interest to instructors and makes a very useful 'notice board' for the association. There is a regional system of organisation which arranges regular meetings, and an annual conference is held at a selected venue each spring. This is the main event of the MSA year.

A flourishing insurance division deals with all classes of insurance, including, of course, car insurance, and there is a 'security plan' to provide cover for instructors in sickness or adversity.

Membership display certificates are issued on admission, and a windscreen certificate for display in the car is issued as a

129

receipt for subscriptions. Members are also encouraged to display MSA car plates, which are supplied at cost and bear the MSA emblem.

It is possible that there will be some slight increase in fees, as, owing to the general financial situation of the country as a whole, a motion is to be put forward at the 1978 annual conference seeking an increase of £5.00 in each category.

Other suggestions which may come to fruition in due course include a revision of the current gradings and a new qualification for members based upon attendance at training courses; certificates are envisaged in 'grades', and the first grade would require attendance at the staff instructor's course. Other grades, yet to be defined, could require a City & Guilds 730 'teacher's certificate', whilst yet another could be for those holding both certificates. If these are implemented, there are further suggestions for a plan to classify members by issuing different coloured certificates, black, blue, green, red and gold, indicating the number of qualifications held by the recipient.

Details of current rules and regulations governing membership and application forms, copies of the code of conduct for instructors and a brochure may be obtained from:

The Director General
The Motor Schools Association of Great Britain
Criterion House
74 Albert Road
Plymouth
PL2 1AF

Notes and References

1   What became known as the 'Emancipation Act' was passed in 1896. It recognised a new class of 'light locomotive', ie under 3 tons and which required fewer than three persons to man it. This act 'legalised' motoring, and permitted vehicles to travel at up to 12 mph. A run of the new 'horseless carriages', to Brighton from London, was immediately organised, and has been religiously repeated ever since each year, with the exception of the war years.

2   Many professional drivers and instructors feel strongly that the advanced tests of all three advanced driving organisations should be officially recognised by the DoT and by all insurance companies. At the moment, although there are several insurance companies who recognise certain of the advanced tests, there is no consistency whatever in their policy between one company and another. Some recognise one advanced organisation, some another, but there seems no hope of all insurance companies recognising all the advanced organisations and rewarding those of their clients who pass any one of the advanced tests with a reduction in premium.

3   There is another symptom which indicates worn wheel bearings, albeit somewhat obscure to many drivers. If your car is fitted with disc brakes, and these feel spongy even after bleeding, then there is a likelihood that worn wheel bearings are causing what is known to mechanics as 'runout'; laymen know it as wobble, and it causes the discs to push the pistons back into their cylinders, thus needing a larger pedal travel than usual for adequate brake application.

4   Although left-hand drive cars are standard on the continent, it is of interest to note that almost until 1960 most of the very expensive ones were fitted with right-hand drive, indeed the famous Bugattis always had right-hand drive. It is believed that Benz was the first to introduce left-hand drive at the turn of the century, while Lancia only changed over to LHD in 1956 as a result of their growing export market to America. There, of course, nearly all manufacturers standardised on LHD around the outbreak of World War I, but the Rolls-Royces built at Springfield between 1921 and 1923 were RHD.

Lanchesters were the first British cars offered with the option of LHD.

5   S. F. Edge was the moving spirit behind Napier; he pioneered the change from tiller to wheel steering and was an early advocate of the 6-cylinder engine. He gained the first international victory for Britain with his Napier in 1902, and was also the centre figure in a stormy discussion concerning the Rudge-Whitworth detachable wheel. He was fastest with his 80 hp Napier in the first speed hillclimb in the Isle of Man in 1904, and celebrated the opening of the old Brooklands Track in 1907 with a twenty-four hour run, establishing a record which stood until 1924.

Charles Jarrott, who gave up a law career for racing, was a London agent for Oldsmobile (which then cost £150). He was the first driver ever to wear British racing green, allocated to him in the Gordon Bennett Race of 1900 to offset his 'unlucky' number 13. This race was the first one in which international racing colours were used. He earned a reputation for always finishing any competition he had started, even to the extent of repairing his cars with wood from hotel furniture, and frequently finished races with bits and pieces missing.

Addresses of Useful Authorities, Clubs and Organisations

The Automobile Association,
Fanum House, Leicester Square, London WC2

Association of Scottish Motorists,
30 Hillview Drive, Clarkston, Renfrewshire

Auto Camping Club,
5 Dunsfold Rise, Coulsdon, Surrey

British Automobile Racing Club,
Sutherland House, 5-6 Argyll Street, London W1

British Racing and Sports Car Club,
Empire House, Chiswick High Road, London W4

British Tourist Authority,
64 St James Street, London SW1

Camping Club of Great Britain and Ireland Ltd,
11 Lower Grosvenor Place, London SW1

Caravan Club,
65 South Molton Street, London W1Y 2AB

Countryside Club,
109 Upper Woodcote Road, Caversham Heights, Reading, Berks

Disabled Drivers Motor Club Ltd,
36a Woodfield Road, Ealing, London W5

English Tourist Board,
4 Grosvenor Gardens, London SW1

Europ-Assistance Ltd,
269 High Street, Croydon, Surrey CR0 1QH

Forces Motoring Club,
12 Bowling Green Lane, London EC1

Forestry Commission,
25 Savile Row, London W1

French Chamber of Commerce,
196 Sloane Street, London SW1X 9QX

Guernsey Tourist Committee,
PO Box 23, Guernsey

Guild of Lady Drivers,
413a Brixton Road, London W9

Heart of England Tourist Board,
PO Box 15, Worcester WR1 2JT

Highlands and Islands Development Board,
PO Box 7, Bridge House, Bank Street, Inverness

Institute of Advanced Motorists,
Empire House, Chiswick High Road, London W4

Isle of Man Tourist Board,
13 Victoria Street, Douglas, Isle of Man

Isle of Wight Tourist Board,
21 High Street, Newport, Isle of Wight

Jersey Tourism Committee,
Weighbridge, St Helier, Jersey

League of Safe Drivers,
17 Holmwood Gardens, London N3 3NS

Manx Automobile Club,
8 Mill Street, Douglas, Isle of Man

Midland Automobile Club,
4 Vicarage Road, Ivy Bush, Edgbaston, Birmingham 15

Midland Car Club,
12 Cherry Street, Birmingham 2

Motor Schools Association,
Atherton House, 12 Tilton Street, London SW6 7LR

National Advanced Drivers' Association,
2 Queensway, Sawston, Cambridge CB2 4DJ

National Press Automobile Association,
5 Folkington Corner, Woodside Park, Finchley, London N12

National Trust for Places of Historic Interest and Natural Beauty,
42 Queen Annes Gate, London SW1

Northern Ireland Tourist Board,
River House, High Street, Belfast BT1 2DS

Order of the Road,
55 Park Lane, London W1

Overseas Drivers Club,
36 Roe Lane, Southport, Lancashire

Parc National de Pyrenees,
Mission de L'Environment Rural et Urbain,
14 Bd du Marechal Leclerc, Neuilly

Recreation and Tourist Committee,
States Office, Alderney

Register of Approved Driving Instructors,
Department of Transport, 2 Marsham Street, London SW1P 3EB

Routiers, Les,
354 Fulham Road, London WS10 9UH

Royal Automobile Club,
83-5 Pall Mall, London SW1Y 5HW

Royal Automobile Club (Motor Sport Division),
31 Belgrave Square, London SW1X 8QH

Scottish Tourist Office,
2 Rutland Place, Edinburgh

Swiss National Tourist Office,
Swiss Centre, New Coventry Street, London W1V 3HG

Thames and Chilterns Tourist Board,
PO Box 10, 8 The Market Place, Abingdon, Oxfordshire OX14 3HG

Trailer Caravan Club,
38 Court Parade, East Lane, Wembley, Middlesex

Touring Club de France,
65 Avenue de Grand Armee, 758782 Paris Cedex 16

Wales Tourist Office,
3 Castle Street, Cardiff

Further Reading

Advanced Driving, the IAM manual (Queen Anne Press)

Cowan, Andrew *Why Finish Last?* (Queen Anne Press, 1969)

Denny, Ronald D. *The Truth About Breath Tests* (Nelson)

Filby, P. J. *Specialist Sports Cars* (David & Charles, 1974)

Flower, Raymond *Motor Sports* (Collins, 1975)

Gibbs, Anthony *Passion For Cars* (David & Charles, 1974)

Harding, Anthony ed. *Car Facts And Feats* (Guinness Superlatives Ltd, 1971)

Hoskin, M. J. *Sensible Driving* (David & Charles, 1974)

Hunt, James. *Against All Odds* (Hamlyn, 1977)

Kells, Joe *Learner Driver* (David & Charles, 1975)

Niekirk, Paul H. *Motoring Offences* (Butterworth, 1972)

Parry, Meyer H. *Aggression On The Road* (Tavistock Publications)

Posthumous, Cyril *British Competition Cars* (Queen Anne Press)

Sheldon, Paul *Milestones Behind The Marques* (David & Charles, 1976)

Stewart, Jackie *Owner-Driver Book* (Pelham Books, 1973)

Walls, A. J. and Brownlie, A. R. *Drink, Drugs And Driving* (Sweet & Maxwell)

Williams, Charles *Car Conversions For Power And Speed* (David & Charles, 1971)

Acknowledgements

The publishers and author wish to offer their sincere thanks to the following for their ungrudging assistance in the preparation of this book, and in particular to the individuals named, without whose assistance it would have been impossible to obtain many of the facts and figures quoted: the Royal Automobile Club, which examines and registers driving instructors, issues competition licences and is the governing body for motor sport in Britain and, in particular, Col J. B. Cowan, Manager, Register of Instructors; the Department of Transport and, in particular, Mrs L. Briggs; Mr D. W. Grime, General Secretary, National Advanced Drivers Association; Mr R. B. Peters, Chief Executive and General Secretary, Institute of Advanced Motorists; Mrs L. Duncan, Organising Secretary, the League of Safe Drivers; Mr H. P. C. Murphy, F Inst MTD, Director General, The Motor Schools Association of Great Britain Limited; Miss M. R. Pierce, Administrative Secretary, BSM High Performance Course; the Automobile Association; the Austin Morris Group of British Leyland; the Royal Society for the Prevention of Accidents.

Index